PRAISE FOR *IT'S OK THAT YOU'RE NOT OK*

"*It's OK That You're Not OK* is a permission slip to feel what you feel, do what you do, and say what you say, when life finds you in a place of profound loss and the world seems hell-bent on telling you the right way to get back to being the person you'll never again be."

JONATHAN FIELDS
author of *How to Live a Good Life*, founder of Good Life Project

"Megan Devine has captured the grief experience: grief is not a problem to be solved, but a mystery to be honored. She understands the pain that grieving people carry *on top* of their actual grief, including the pain of being judged, dismissed, and misunderstood. *It's OK That You're Not OK* is the book I've been waiting for for 30 years—the one I can recommend to any newly bereaved parent, widow, widower, or adult grieving a death."

DONNA SCHUURMAN
senior director of advocacy and training at the
Dougy Center for Grieving Children & Families

"In this beautifully written offering for our broken hearts, Megan Devine antidotes the culture's messed-up messages about bearing the unbearable. We don't have to apologize for being sad! Grief is not a disease from which we must be cured as soon as possible! Rather, the landscape of loss is one of the holiest spaces we can enter. Megan serves as our fearless, feisty, and profoundly compassionate guide."

MIRABAI STARR
translator of *Dark Night of the Soul: John of the Cross* and author
of *Caravan of No Despair: A Memoir of Loss and Transformation*

D0370285

"This book is POWERFUL. Too many grief books focus on 'getting over it,' but this book says: 'Look grief in the eye. Sit with it.' *It's OK That You're Not OK* comes at grief with no flinching. It's intelligent and honest. It's a message that everyone who has ever dealt with loss needs to read."

THERESA REED
author of *The Tarot Coloring Book*

"Our current cultural norms surrounding death render us incapable of dealing with grief authentically and result in unknowingly causing more hurt and suffering to not only ourselves, but the people we care about most. *It's OK That You're Not OK* is the perfect how-to manual to help heal and support ourselves, each other, and our death-avoidant society."

SARAH CHAVEZ
executive director of the Order of the Good Death

"Megan Devine knows grief intimately: she's a therapist and a widow. In this wonderfully honest and deeply generous book, Devine confronts the reality of grieving and reminds us that 'love is the thing that lasts.'"

JESSICA HANDLER
author of *Invisible Sisters: A Memoir* and *Braving the Fire: A Guide to Writing About Grief and Loss*

"*It's OK That You're Not OK* is a wise and necessary book. Megan Devine offers a loving, holistic, and honest vision of what it means to 'companion each other inside what hurts.'"

STEVE EDWARDS
author of *Breaking into the Backcountry*

"This book is the radical take on grief we all need. Megan Devine breaks apart stereotypes and societal expectations that layer additional suffering on top of the intense heartbreak of loss. For those in grief, these words will bring comfort and a deep sense of recognition. With precise language, insightful reflections, and easy-to-implement suggestions, this book is a flashlight for finding a way in the darkest times. For anyone looking to support others in their grief, this is required reading!"

JANA DECRISTOFARO
coordinator of Children's Grief Services,
the Dougy Center for Grieving Children & Families

"Megan Devine's hard-won wisdom has the power to normalize and validate the experience of grief. If you're tired of being asked, 'Are you better now?' read this book for a fresh perspective."

CHRIS GUILLEBEAU
New York Times bestselling author of *The Happiness of Pursuit*

"Grief support and understanding that is heartfelt, straightforward, and wise."

JACK KORNFIELD
author of *A Path with Heart*

IT'S
OK
THAT YOU'RE
NOT
OK

IT'S
OK
THAT YOU'RE
NOT
OK

Meeting Grief and Loss
in a Culture That
Doesn't Understand

MEGAN DEVINE

sounds true
Boulder, Colorado

Sounds True
Boulder, CO 80306

This book is not intended as a substitute for the medical recommendations of physicians, mental health professionals, or other health care providers. Rather, it is intended to offer information to help the reader cooperate with physicians, mental health professionals, and health providers in a mutual request for optimum well-being. We advise readers to carefully review and understand the ideas presented and to seek the advice of a qualified professional before attempting to use them.

Some names and identifying details have been changed to protect the privacy of individuals.

Published 2017

Cover design by Rachael Murray
Book design by Beth Skelley

Printed in the United States of America

Library of Congress Cataloging-in-Publication Data
Names: Devine, Megan, author.
Title: It's ok that you're not ok : meeting grief and loss in a culture that doesn't understand / Megan Devine.
Description: Boulder, CO : Sounds True, [2018] | Includes bibliographical references. | Description based on print version record and CIP data provided by publisher; resource not viewed.
Identifiers: LCCN 2017004709 (print) | LCCN 2017020725 (ebook) | ISBN 9781622039081 (ebook) | ISBN 9781622039074 (pbk.)
Subjects: LCSH: Grief. | Loss (Psychology)
Classification: LCC BF575.G7 (ebook) | LCC BF575.G7 D479 2018 (print) | DDC 155.9/3—dc23
LC record available at https://lccn.loc.gov/2017004709

For those who are the stuff of other people's nightmares.

Exposed to all that is lost, she sings with a stray girl who is also herself, her amulet.

ALEJANDRA PIZARNIK

For small creatures such as we the vastness is bearable only through love.

CARL SAGAN

CONTENTS

FOREWORD

There is a twin paradox in being human. First, no one can live your life for you—no one can face what is yours to face or feel what is yours to feel—*and* no one can make it alone. Secondly, in living our one life, we are here to love and lose. No one knows why. It is just so. If we commit to loving, we will inevitably know loss and grief. If we try to avoid loss and grief, we will never truly love. Yet powerfully and mysteriously, knowing both love and loss is what brings us fully and deeply alive.

Having known love and loss deeply, Megan Devine is a strong and caring companion. Having lost a loved one, she knows that life is forever changed. There is no getting over it, but only getting under it. Loss and grief change our landscape. The terrain is forever different and there is no normal to return to. There is only the inner task of making a new and accurate map. As Megan so wisely says, "We're not here to fix our pain, but to tend to it."

The truth is that those who suffer carry a wisdom that the rest of us need. And given that we live in a society that is afraid to feel, it's important to open each other to the depth of the human journey, which can only be known through the life of our feelings.

Ultimately, the true bond of love and friendship is knit by how much we can experience love and loss together, without judging or pushing each other; not letting each other drown in the deep or rescuing each other from the baptism of soul that waits there. As Megan affirms, "Real safety is in entering each other's pain, [and] recognizing ourselves inside it."

Our work, alone and together, is not to minimize the pain or loss we feel, but to investigate what these life-changing incidents are opening in us. I have learned through my own pain and grief that to be broken is no reason to see all things as broken. And so, the gift and practice of being human centers on the effort to restore what matters and, when in trouble, to make good use of our heart.

Like John of the Cross, who faced the dark night of the soul, and like Jacob, who wrestled the nameless angel in the bottom of the ravine, Megan lost her partner Matt and wrestled through a long dark ravine. And the truth she arrives with is not that everything will be alright or repaired or forgotten. But that things will evolve and root as real, that those who suffer great loss will be inextricably woven with life again, though everything will change.

In Dante's *Divine Comedy*, Virgil is Dante's guide through hell into purgatory, right up until Dante faces a wall of flame, which he balks at, afraid. But Virgil tells him, "You have no choice. It is the fire that will burn but not consume." Dante is still afraid. Sensing this, Virgil puts his hand on his shoulder and repeats, "You have no choice." Dante then summons his courage and enters.

Everyone who lives comes upon this wall of fire. Like Virgil, Megan is a guide through hell, up to the wall of fire we each must pass through alone, beyond which we become our own guides. Like Virgil, Megan points out a way, not *the* way, but a way, offering those in the mad turmoil of grief a few things to hold onto. It is courageous work to love and lose and keep each other company, no matter how long the road. And Megan is a courageous teacher. If you are in the grip of grief, reach for this book. It will help you carry what is yours to carry while making the journey less alone.

Mark Nepo

ACKNOWLEDGMENTS

I always read the dedications and acknowledgments in a book. I like to see the relationship lines, the mentors and guides, the life that surrounds the book, and the one who wrote it. A book is a tiny fragment of a life, and a by-product of it. They inter-feed, which is a weird way to put it. This book was hard for me, and beautiful, in ways that aren't always clear on the page but were clearly held by the people in my life. Samantha (who held everything), Cynthia, Rosie, TC, Steph, Michael, Sarah, Naga, Wit, and another handful of people who came in and out of this time—thank you for being there, for listening, and for digging me out when I got lost. To my twin loves, who during the writing of this book were my play, my adventure, my respite, and my joy—for as long as it lasts, and beyond, thank you. Thank you to my tango community, for being the one consistent place I could stop writing, even in my head. My writing students, for so many reasons, are the backbone of this book, their emails and notes often coming at just the right moment to remind me why I do this work. Thank you, my loves, for sharing your hearts and your words with me. To my friends and allies who died in the years since Matt's death, I still feel you around me. Then, as now, your support means more than worlds to me. Thank you to my agent, David Fugate, who believed in the message of cultural transformation from the moment we first talked about grief. And to my team at Sounds True, as I've told you before, I feel loved and cared for by you, and that is everything. Thank you.

And though it seems strange, or maybe arrogant, I owe an unending thank-you to myself—to the person I was, the person at the river that day and in the years soon after, the one who lived when she did not want to. This book is a love letter back to her, an act of time travel. In so many ways, through this book, I want for myself what I want for all who read it—to reach back with my words, to hold her, to help her survive. I am so glad she lived.

INTRODUCTION

The way we deal with grief in our culture is broken. I thought I knew quite a bit about grief. After all, I'd been a psychotherapist in private practice for nearly a decade. I worked with hundreds of people—from those wrestling with substance addiction and patterns of homelessness to private practice clients facing decades-old abuse, trauma, and grief. I'd worked in sexual violence education and advocacy, helping people navigate some of the most horrific experiences of their lives. I studied the cutting edge of emotional literacy and resilience. I cared deeply and felt that I was doing important, valuable work.

And then, on a beautiful, ordinary summer day in 2009, I watched my partner drown. Matt was strong, fit, and healthy. He was just three months away from his fortieth birthday. With his abilities and experience, there was no reason he should have drowned. It was random, unexpected, and it tore my world apart.

After Matt died, I wanted to call every one of my clients and apologize for my ignorance. Though I'd been skilled in deep emotional work, Matt's death revealed an entirely different world. None of what I knew applied to loss of that magnitude. With all my experience and training, if anyone could be prepared to deal with that kind of loss, it should've been me.

But nothing could have prepared me for that. None of what I'd learned mattered.

And I wasn't alone.

In the first years after Matt's death, I slowly discovered a community of grieving people. Writers, activists, professors, social workers, and scientists in our professional worlds, our small band of young widows and parents grieving the loss of young children came together in our shared experience of pain. But it wasn't just loss that we shared. Every one of us had felt judged, shamed, and corrected in our grief. We shared stories of being encouraged to "get over it," put the past behind us, and stop talking about those we had lost. We were admonished to move on with our lives and told we needed these deaths in order to learn what was important in life. Even those who tried to help ended up hurting. Platitudes and advice, even when said with good intentions, came across as dismissive, reducing such great pain to greeting card one-liners.

At a time when we most needed love and support, each one of us felt alone, misunderstood, judged, and dismissed. It's not that the people around us meant to be cruel; they just didn't know how to be truly helpful. Like many grieving people, we stopped talking about our pain to friends and family. It was easier to pretend everything was fine than to continually defend and explain our grief to those who couldn't understand. We turned to other grieving people because they were the only ones who knew what grief was really like.

Grief and loss happen to everyone. We've all felt misunderstood during times of great pain. We've also stood by, helpless, in the face of other people's pain. We've all fumbled for words, knowing no words can ever make things right. No one can win: grieving people feel misunderstood, and friends and family feel helpless and stupid in the face of grief. We know we need help, but we don't really know what to ask for. Trying to help, we actually make it worse for people going through the worst time in their lives. Our best intentions come out garbled.

It's not our fault. We all want to feel loved and supported in our times of grief, and we all want to help those we love. The problem is that we've been taught the wrong way to do it.

Our culture sees grief as a kind of malady: a terrifying, messy emotion that needs to be cleaned up and put behind us as soon as possible. As a result, we have outdated beliefs around how long grief should last and what it should look like. We see it as something to overcome, something to fix, rather than something to tend or support. Even our clinicians are trained to see grief as a disorder rather than a natural response to deep loss. When the professionals don't know how to handle grief, the rest of us can hardly be expected to respond with skill and grace.

There's a gap, a great divide between what we most want and where we are now. The tools we currently have for dealing with grief are not going to bridge that gap. Our cultural and professional ideas about what grief should look like keep us from caring for ourselves inside grief, and they keep us from being able to support those we love. Even worse, those outdated ideas add unnecessary suffering on top of natural, normal pain.

There is another way.

Since Matt's death, I've worked with thousands of grieving people through my website, Refuge in Grief. I've spent the past years acquiring expertise about what truly helps during the long slog of grief. Along the way, I've established myself as a nationally known, leading voice not only in grief support but in a more compassionate, skillful way of relating to one another.

My theories on grief, vulnerability, and emotional literacy have been drawn from my own experience and the stories and experiences of the thousands of people trying their best to make their way through the landscape of grief. From grieving people themselves, and from friends and family members struggling to support them, I've identified the real problem: our culture simply hasn't taught us how to come to grief with the skills needed to be truly helpful.

If we want to care for one another better, we have to rehumanize grief. We have to talk about it. We have to understand it as a natural, normal process, rather than something to be shunned, rushed, or maligned. We have to start talking about the real skills needed to face the reality of living a life entirely changed by loss.

It's OK That You're Not OK provides a new way of looking at grief—a new model offered not by some professor locked up in an office, *studying* grief, but by someone who's lived it. I've been inside that grief. I've been the person howling on the floor, unable to eat or to sleep, unable to tolerate leaving the house for more than a few minutes at a time. I've been on the other side of the clinician's couch, on the receiving end of outdated and wholly irrelevant talk of stages and the power of positive thinking. I've struggled with the physical aspects of grief (memory loss, cognitive changes, anxiety) and found tools that help. With a combination of my clinical skills and my own experience, I learned the difference between *solving* pain and *tending* to pain. I learned, firsthand, why trying to talk someone out of their grief is both hurtful and entirely different from helping them live with their grief.

This book provides a path to rethink our relationship with grief. It encourages readers to see their grief as a natural response to death and loss, rather than an aberrant condition needing transformation. By shifting the focus from grief as a problem to be solved to an experience to be tended, we give the reader what we most want for ourselves: understanding, compassion, validation, and a way through the pain.

It's OK That You're Not OK shows readers how to live with skill and compassion during their grief, but it isn't just a book for people in pain: this book is about making things better for everyone. All of us are going to experience deep grief or loss at some point in our lives. All of us are going to know someone living great loss. Loss is a universal experience.

In a world that tells us that grieving the death of someone you love is an illness needing treatment, this book offers a different perspective, a perspective that encourages us to reexamine our relationship with love, loss, heartbreak, and community. If we can start to understand the true nature of grief, we can have a more helpful, loving, supportive culture. We can get what we *all* most want: to help each other in our moments of need, to feel loved and supported no matter what horrors erupt in our lives. When we change our conversations around grief, we make things better for everyone.

What we all share in common—the real reason for this book—is a desire to love better. To love ourselves in the midst of great pain, and to love one another when the pain of this life grows too large for one person to hold. This book offers the skills needed to make that kind of love a reality.

Thank you for being here. For being willing to read, to listen, to learn. Together, we can make things better, even when we can't make them right.

PART I

THIS IS ALL JUST AS

CRAZY

AS YOU THINK IT IS

1

THE REALITY OF LOSS

Here's what I most want you to know: this really is as bad as you think.

No matter what anyone else says, this sucks. What has happened cannot be made right. What is lost cannot be restored. There is no beauty here, inside this central fact.

Acknowledgment is everything.

You're in pain. It can't be made better.

The reality of grief is far different from what others see from the outside. There is pain in this world that you can't be cheered out of.

You don't need solutions. You don't need to move on from your grief. You need someone to see your grief, to acknowledge it. You need someone to hold your hands while you stand there in blinking horror, staring at the hole that was your life.

Some things cannot be fixed. They can only be carried.

THE REALITY OF GRIEF

When out-of-order death or a life-altering event enters your life, everything changes. Even when it's expected, death or loss still comes as a surprise. Everything is different now. The life you expected to unfold disappears: vaporized. The world splits open, and nothing makes sense. Your life was normal, and now, suddenly, it's anything but normal. Otherwise intelligent people have started spouting slogans and platitudes, trying to cheer you up. Trying to take away your pain.

■ ■ ■

This is not how you thought it would be.

Time has stopped. Nothing feels real. Your mind cannot stop replaying the events, hoping for a different outcome. The ordinary, everyday world that others still inhabit feels coarse and cruel. You can't eat (or you eat everything). You can't sleep (or you sleep all the time). Every object in your life becomes an artifact, a symbol of the life that used to be and might have been. There is no place this loss has not touched.

In the days and weeks since your loss, you've heard all manner of things about your grief: They wouldn't want you to be sad. Everything happens for a reason. At least you had them as long as you did. You're strong and smart and resourceful—you'll get through this! This experience will make you stronger. You can always try again—get another partner, have another child, find some way to channel your pain into something beautiful and useful and good.

Platitudes and cheerleading solve nothing. In fact, this kind of support only makes you feel like no one in the world understands. This isn't a paper cut. It's not a crisis of confidence. You didn't need this thing to happen in order to know what's important, to find your calling, or even to understand that you are, in fact, deeply loved.

Telling the truth about grief is the only way forward: your loss is exactly as bad as you think it is. And people, try as they might, really are responding to your loss as poorly as you think they are. You aren't crazy. Something crazy has happened, and you're responding as any sane person would.

WHAT'S THE PROBLEM?

Most of what passes for grief support these days is less than useful. Because we don't talk about loss, most people—and many professionals—think of grief and loss as aberrations, detours from a normal, happy life.

We believe that the goal of grief support, personal or professional, is to get out of grief, to stop feeling pain. Grief is something to get through as quickly as possible. An unfortunate, but fleeting, experience that is best sorted and put behind you.

It's that faulty belief that leaves so many grieving people feeling alone and abandoned on top of their grief. There's so much correction and judgment inside grief; many feel it's just easier to not talk about what hurts. Because we don't talk about the reality of loss, many grieving people think that what's happening to them is strange, or weird, or wrong.

There is nothing wrong with grief. It's a natural extension of love. It's a healthy and sane response to loss. That grief feels bad doesn't make it bad; that you feel crazy doesn't mean you are crazy.

Grief is part of love. Love for life, love for self, love for others. What you are living, painful as it is, is love. And love is really hard. Excruciating at times.

If you're going to feel this experience as part of love, we need to start talking about it in real terms, not as pathology, and not with some false hope of everything working out alright in the end.

GRIEF BEYOND "NORMAL" GRIEF

Everyday life carries losses and grief. There is immense work to be done in our culture around giving everyone a voice, around validating and honoring all the pains we carry in our hearts, all the loss we encounter. But this book isn't about those daily losses.

There are wounds in this life that hurt, that hurt immensely, that can eventually be overcome. Through self-work and hard work, many difficulties can be transformed. There really is gold to be found, as the Jungians say, at the bottom of all the heavy work of life. But this is not one of those times. This isn't a hard day at work. This isn't simply not getting something you deeply, truly wanted. This is not losing something beautiful just so something more "right for you" can come along. The work of transformation does not apply here.

There are losses that rearrange the world. Deaths that change the way you see everything, grief that tears everything down. Pain that transports you to an entirely different universe, even while everyone else thinks nothing has really changed.

When I talk about loss, when I talk about grief, I am talking about things beyond what we consider the natural order of things. I am talking about accidents and illnesses, natural disasters, man-made disasters, violent crimes, and suicides. I'm talking about the random, atypical, unusual losses that seem more and more common as I do this work. I'm talking about the underground losses, the pain no one wants to talk about—or more, no one wants to hear about: The baby who died days before his birth, with no known cause. The athletic, driven young man who dove into a pond and came out paralyzed. The young wife who saw her husband shot in a random carjacking. The partner swept away by a rogue wave. The vibrant, healthy woman whose stage-four cancer was discovered during a routine checkup, leaving a husband, young son, and countless friends within a few months of hearing the news. The twenty-year-old kid struck by a bus while working a humanitarian mission in South America. The family vacationing in Indonesia as the tsunami hit.

The community reeling after a hate crime claimed their friends and families. The young child taken down by a mutation in her bones. The brother, alive and well at breakfast, dead by lunch. The friend whose struggles you did not realize until they were found dead by their own hand.

Maybe you've come here because someone is dead. I'm here because someone is dead. Maybe you've come because life has irrevocably changed—through accident or illness, through violent crime or act of nature.

How random and fragile life can be.

We don't talk about the fragility of life: how everything can be normal one moment, and completely changed the next. We have no words, no language, no capacity to face this, together or as individuals. Because we don't talk about it, when we most need love and support, there's nothing to be found. What *is* available falls far short of what we need.

The reality of grief is different from what others see or guess from the outside. Platitudes and pat explanations will not work here. There is not a reason for everything. Not every loss can be transformed into something useful. Things happen that do not have a silver lining.

We have to start telling the truth about this kind of pain. About grief, about love, about loss.

Because the truth is, in one way or another, loving each other means losing each other. Being alive in such a fleeting, tenuous world is hard. Our hearts get broken in ways that can't be fixed. There is pain that becomes an immovable part of our lives. We need to know how to endure that, how to care for ourselves inside that, how to care for one another. We need to know how to live here, where life as we know it can change, forever, at any time.

We need to start talking about *that* reality of life, which is also the reality of love.

SURVIVAL

If you've found yourself here, in this life you didn't ask for, in this life you didn't see coming, I'm sorry. I can't tell you it will all work out in the end. I can't tell you things will be just fine.

You are not "OK." You might not ever be "OK."

Whatever grief you're carrying, it's important to acknowledge how bad this is, how hard. It really is horrendous, horrifying, and unsurvivable.

This book is not about fixing you, or fixing your grief. It's not about making you "better" or getting you back to "normal." This book is about how you live inside your loss. How you carry what cannot be fixed. How you survive.

And even though that thought—that you *can* survive something as horrifying as this—is unsettling and horrifying in its own right, the truth is, you will most likely survive.

Your survival in this life post-loss won't follow steps or stages, or align with anyone else's vision of what life might be for you. Survival won't be found, can't be found, in easy answers or in putting your lost life behind you, pretending you didn't really want it anyway.

In order to survive, to find that life that feels authentic and true to you, we have to start with telling the truth. This really is as bad as you think. Everything really is as wrong, and as bizarre, as you know it to be. When we start there, we can begin to talk about living with grief, living inside the love that remains.

HOW TO USE THIS BOOK

It's OK That You're Not OK is divided into four parts: the reality of loss, what to do with your grief, friends and family, and the way forward. Throughout this book, you'll find excerpts from students in my Writing Your Grief courses. Their words, often even more so than my own, illustrate the challenging and multifaceted aspects of grief lived honestly and openly.

While the book progresses in a somewhat linear fashion, jump around however you see fit. As with grief, there's no right way to explore this. Especially in early grief, there's only so much you can absorb. Even if you had a deep attention span before your loss, grief has a way of shortening that considerably. Take things in manageable chunks. (I discuss more on how grief affects your brain and body in part 2.)

The first part of the book is about the culture of grief and how we come to pain like yours. It dives into the historical roots of emotional illiteracy, of our deep aversion to facing the realities of pain. It's the wide view of grief, the view of what grief—and love—looks like when seen through a much longer lens.

If your world has just imploded, why should you care about the wider view? Why should you spend any time at all reflecting on how emotionally illiterate this world is?

Well, it's true: cultural understandings of grief don't really matter in the early days. What does matter is knowing that you aren't alone in feeling like the world at large has failed you. Discussions of the way we deal with grief in this culture can help you feel less alone. They can validate the crazy dissonance between your reality and the reality others foist on you.

That difference between what the outside world believes and what you know to be true can be one of the hardest aspects of grief.

I remember my own early days after my partner drowned—shoving myself out into the world, frazzled hair, sunken cheeks, mismatched clothes, looking for all the world like a homeless woman, babbling on to myself. Trying to keep moving. Doing what was reasonable, expected, ordinary: groceries, dog walks, meeting friends for lunch. Nodding back at people who told me everything was going to be OK. Holding my tongue, being polite, when therapist after therapist told me I had to progress through the stages of grief more quickly.

All the while, beside me, inside me, was the howling, shrieking, screaming mass of pain, watching this normal and ordinary person being reasonable. Polite. As though anything was OK. As though what I was living was not that bad. As though horror could be managed through acceptable behavior.

I could see the fault lines running through everything, knowing that all these reasonable people talking to me about stages of grief, about pushing myself through the pain to some exalted vision of "getting better," all the books that pointed toward getting out of pain by simply rising above it somehow—I knew it was crap. Saying so only got me labeled as "resistant."

What I would have given to see my reality reflected back to me. Grief support is kind of like the emperor's new clothes of the relational world—those in pain know that what passes for support is truly nothing at all, while well-intentioned support people continue to spout off empty encouragement and worn-out platitudes, knowing in their hearts that those words don't help at all. We all know this, and yet no one says anything.

How irrelevant it is to talk about grief as though it were an intellectual exercise, something you can simply use your mind to rise above. The intelligence that arranges words and dictates stages or steps or reasonable behavior is on a wholly different plane than the heart that is newly smashed open.

Grief is visceral, not reasonable: the howling at the center of grief is raw and real. It is love in its most wild form. The first part of this book explores our cultural and historical reluctance to feel that wildness. While it won't change anything inside your loss, hearing your personal experience set against the wider, broken culture can help shift things somehow.

The second part of this book is what you can actually do inside your grief—not to make it "better," but to help you withstand the life you are called to live. Just because you can't fix grief doesn't mean there is nothing you can do inside it. When we shift the focus from fixing your pain to simply tending to it, a whole world of support opens up. Validation and frank discussion of the realities of grief makes things different, even when it can't make things "right."

Part 2 explores some of the most common, and least discussed, aspects of grief, including the mental and physical changes that come with intense loss. There are exercises to help you manage unnecessary or unavoidable stress, improve your sleep, decrease anxiety, deal with intrusive or repetitive images related to your loss, and find tiny windows of calm where things aren't all better, but they are somewhat easier to carry.

In part 3, we explore the often frustrating and occasionally amazing support from friends, family, and acquaintances surrounding you. How is it possible that otherwise intelligent, insightful people have no idea how to truly support you inside your loss? While we can't fault those with "good intentions," it's simply not enough to say they mean well. How do you help those who want to help you? My hope is that you'll use the third part of this book to do just that: hand it over to those who truly want to be of help, and let this book guide the way. There are checklists, suggestions, and first-person essays to help your support teams be more skilled in how they come to your pain. And just as important, part 3 helps you figure out who simply can't be there for you, and how to cut them from your life with at least *some* skill and grace.

The last part of this book looks at ways we move forward after devastating loss. Given that your loss is not something to be fixed, what would "living a good life" even look like? How do you live here, in a world that is so completely changed? It's a complex and complicated process—carrying love with you, moving forward as opposed to "moving on." Part 4 dives into the ways we find true support and companionship inside loss, and the ways that pain—and love—get integrated into a life lived alongside loss.

And that's the truth about grief: loss gets integrated, not overcome. However long it takes, your heart and your mind will carve out a new life amid this weirdly devastated landscape. Little by little, pain and love will find ways to coexist. It won't feel wrong or bad to have survived. It will be, simply, a life of your own making: the most beautiful life it can be, given what is yours to live. May this book help you find the thread of love that still exists, following it forward into a life you didn't ask for, but is here nonetheless.

I'm so sorry you have need of this book, and I'm so glad you're here.

2

THE SECOND HALF
OF THE SENTENCE

Why Words of Comfort
Feel So Bad

It's incredibly hard to watch someone you love in pain. Those who love you tell you you're strong enough to get through this. You'll feel better someday. It won't always be this bad. They encourage you to look to your much brighter future, to a time when you aren't in so much pain.

People offer suggestions for how to get out of your grief faster. They tell you what they would do if they were in your position. They tell you about their own losses, as though every grief is exactly the same. As though knowing someone else has suffered makes anything any different.

From close friends to casual acquaintances, everyone has a take on your grief; everyone wants to make it better for you somehow.

Of course people want to make you feel better—it's part of being human: We want to take away what hurts. We want to help. We want to *be* helped. We want things from each other we should be able to give. But instead of feeling held and comforted, many grieving people feel shamed, shunned, and dismissed.

Instead of feeling effective and useful, those trying to help feel unwanted, frustrated, and unappreciated.

No one gets what they want.

Most of this part of the book focuses on our messed-up cultural models around grief and pain, but this chapter stays personal: it's important to validate how crazy other people's responses to your loss can make you feel. Wondering if other people are nuts or you're just being "too sensitive" adds an additional level of stress. Validation and acknowledgment are important—there really is something not comforting in the way people are trying to comfort you.

THEIR WORDS SEEM OK: SO WHY DO THEY MAKE ME SO ANGRY?

A very dear friend of mine's father died during the time I was writing this book. She sent me a text about a week after he died: "People are sending me the sweetest condolence cards. Why does this make me so enraged? I hate them and their stupid cards. Even the nicest words seem mean."

Intense grief is an impossibility: there is no "making it better." Words of intended comfort just grate. "Help" from other people feels like an intrusion. Attempts at connection or understanding come across as clueless or rude. Everyone has an opinion as to how you should be grieving and how you can make this better for yourself. Platitudes about coming through this "even stronger" and admonishments to "remember the good times" feel like a slap in the face.

Why do words of comfort feel so horribly wrong?

Before my partner died, I was reading *There Is a Spiritual Solution to Every Problem* by Dr. Wayne Dyer. It's a great book. When I tried to pick it up after Matt died, though, I couldn't get back into it. It just kept feeling wrong, like there was a burr inside the words that scratched uncomfortably. I kept trying to find comfort in the words I found comforting and helpful before, and those words were just not doing it.

I put the book down. I picked it back up. The burr rasped and the words didn't fit, and I put the book back down.

It was several weeks later when my eye happened to catch the title of the book as it lay on the coffee table: there's a spiritual solution to every problem.

Every *problem*.

Suddenly, it made sense. There may in fact be a spiritual solution to every problem, but grief is not a problem to be solved. It isn't "wrong," and it can't be "fixed." It isn't an illness to be cured.

We assume that if something is uncomfortable, it means something is wrong. People conclude that grief is "bad" because it hurts. We hear about relieving the pain, getting out of pain, dreaming of a time when there is no pain. We behave as though grief is something to get out of as soon as possible, an aberration that needs healing, rather than a natural response to loss.

Most people approach grief as a problem to be solved. Your friends and family see you in pain, and they want to relieve your pain. Whether that aim is stated clearly or not, it's the sole reason why words of comfort usually feel anything but comforting to you in your grief. Intentionally or not, by trying to solve your grief, they aren't giving you the support you actually need.

As I told my friend, those sweet-seeming condolence cards feel offensive because, at their root, they're trying to fix pain. They skip over the true reality of the situation: this hurts. Though they often don't mean to, people make grief feel much worse when they try to pretty it up, gloss over it, or make it go away. Whether comfort and condolences come in person or in those beautiful/awful cards, this chapter goes over some of the ways the best of intentions can backfire.

HEY, ME TOO!

When they hear about your loss, many people will try to empathize by telling you their own grief stories. This ranges from the close-but-no-cigar comparison of "My husband died, too," to "My goldfish died when I was eight, so I know just how you feel."

We share stories of loss to communicate that we understand where you are: "Hey, look. I've walked this road. I understand how you feel."

Shared loss stories are an attempt to make you feel less alone inside your grief. They don't usually land that way, though. Comparing one grief with another almost always backfires. One experience of loss does not translate into another. Grief is as individual as love. That someone has experienced a loss—even one similar to yours—does not mean they understand you.

When someone relates their own story of loss, they're hoping to remove some of your pain. True. But that's not all. Everyone carries grief—from the everyday losses to the bigger, life-altering ones. Because we don't talk about grief in our culture, we have personal and global backlogs of unheard and unspoken grief. When you become visible in your grief, it's like a portal opens, a doorway into acceptability and openness. When you start talking about loss, it's like there's suddenly this permission, and we think, *Oh, thank goodness, we're talking about grief now. Let me tell you about the losses I've suffered!*

We all want to talk about our pain. We all carry stories that need acknowledgment. But right now? Right now, when you are in pain, when your loss is primary and powerful? That is not the time for a two-way, give-and-take discussion about the losses we all sustain.

Grief comparison and shared grief stories do not bring you comfort. Of course they don't.

It can feel like your own loss has been eclipsed by the speaker's need to tell their own story—no matter how long ago it happened, or how irrelevant it is to your loss.

Talking about their own pain is a way the speaker moves the focus off supporting you and onto getting their own needs met. It seems nefarious, but it's just one of the subtle ways our faulty grief culture impacts your actual grieving process.

There is a time and a place to discuss our shared stories of loss. When your world has just imploded is not one of those times. You feel "mugged" by other people's grief stories because something has been taken away from you: the central importance of *your* current reality.

THE COMPETITION OF GRIEF

Sharing grief as a way to connect with the griever almost always turns into a competition of grief: the grief Olympics. Whose pain is worse? Whose grief means more?

If you've told someone that their experience of loss is not the same as yours, I bet you've heard a defensive backlash from them. They're hurt. Offended. If you respond to the speaker's shared grief story by saying, "They aren't the same thing," what they hear is: "Your grief is not as real as mine." They hear that their pain wasn't bad enough. They hear that distinction as an insult to their heart, a dismissal of their pain.

What started out as an attempt to connect devolves into an argument over whose grief hurts more.

We need to talk about the hierarchy of grief. You hear it all the time—no grief is worse than any other. I don't think that's one bit true. There *is* a hierarchy of grief. Divorce is not the same as the death of a partner. Death of a grandparent is not the same as the death of a child. Losing your job is not the same as losing a limb.

Here's the thing: every loss is valid. And every loss is not the same. You can't flatten the landscape of grief and say that everything is equal. It isn't.

It's easier to see when we take it out of the intensely personal: stubbing your toe hurts. It totally hurts. For a moment, the pain can be all-consuming. You might even hobble for a while. Having your foot ripped off by a passing freight train hurts, too. Differently. The pain lasts longer. The injury needs recovery time, which may be uncertain or complicated. It affects and impacts your life moving forward. You can't go back to the life you had before you became a one-footed person. No one would say these two injuries are exactly the same.

A stubbed toe hurts, and it gets to be honored and heard without being dismissed as no big deal. A torn-off foot is different. It gets to be honored and heard without being dismissed. That all grief is valid does not mean that all grief is the same. Ordinary heartbreaks are difficult, even without reordering the world as you know it. Random, out-of-order, life-altering losses have an echo that reverberates in a different way. Not better, not worse—simply not the same.

We need to be careful that we don't exclude anyone's grief. We all deserve to be heard in our grief, no matter what that grief may be. At the same time, we can't assign equal weight to all losses and successfully support someone in pain. Making no distinction between levels of grief does not support the griever.

It's also true that after a certain point, comparisons become useless. Is it worse to lose a child or to lose a partner? Sudden death or long illness? Suicide or murder? Babies die. Children get cancer. Lovers drown. Earthquakes open the seemingly solid ground, and thousands of people disappear. Bombs go off in random places. The seemingly ordered universe is split open into a big yawning chasm, and no reality makes sense anymore. Distinctions between losses like these do not matter, and they are not helpful.

What we need to remember—as a working practice—is to honor all griefs. Honor all losses, small and not small. Life changing and moment changing. And then, not to compare them. That all people experience pain is not medicine for anything.

Defending the uniqueness of your own loss against the comparisons of others is just not going to help you feel better. Pointing out the various orders of magnitude in loss is not going to help you feel better.

When someone tries to alleviate your pain by sharing their own story of suffering, know that they are attempting to connect and relate. And know that there is a reason it feels so crappy: they aren't actually connecting. They're unintentionally turning the focus away from you and onto their own stories of pain. Your reality is erased, which is exactly the opposite of what they'd hoped to do.

It then sets up this "my grief is worse than yours" dichotomy that leaves everyone feeling unheard and dismissed.

Comparison doesn't work for anyone.

THE SECOND HALF OF THE SENTENCE

Even without comparison, words of comfort from other people can still feel horribly wrong.

We've all been on both sides of the "comfort" equation—jumping in with words meant to soothe someone in pain, feeling helpless and awkward and ridiculous, and being on the receiving end of someone else's words, feeling dismissed or patronized rather than comforted. Why do our intentions come out so backward? Why, even when you know they mean well, do the words of other people grate and annoy?

Stepping over some of the more egregious and ridiculously hurtful things people have said (for now), here's a short list of some of the things grieving people have heard from people intending to offer comfort and support:

At least you had them for as long as you did.

You can always have another child/find another partner.

They're in a better place now.

At least now you get to know what's really important in life.

This will make you a better person in the end.

You won't always feel this bad.

You're stronger than you think.

This is all part of the plan.

Everything happens for a reason.

Saying something like "He wouldn't want you to be sad" or "At least you had her for as long as you did" might seem like a comfort. The problem is, there's an implied second half of the sentence in all those familiar lines. That second half of the sentence unintentionally dismisses or diminishes your pain; it erases what is true now in favor of some alternate experience. That ghost-sentence tells you it's not OK to feel how you feel.

TRY THIS

THE SECOND HALF OF THE SENTENCE

For each of these familiar comforting statements, add the phrase "so stop feeling so bad."

At least you had her for as long as you did (so stop feeling so bad).

He died doing something he loved (so stop feeling so bad).

You can always have another child (so stop feeling so bad).

If you cringe or feel angry when friends and family try to comfort you, it's because you hear the second half of that sentence, even when they don't say it out loud. The implication is always there, speaking louder in its own silence: *stop feeling how you feel.*

Friends and family want you to feel better. They want to take away your pain. What they don't understand is that in trying to take your pain away, they're actually dismissing and minimizing the extent of your grief. They aren't seeing your reality for what it is. They don't see you.

Words of comfort that try to erase pain are not a comfort. When you try to take someone's pain away from them, you don't make it better. You just tell them it's not OK to talk about their pain.

To feel truly comforted by someone, you need to feel heard in your pain. You need the reality of your loss reflected back to you—not diminished, not diluted. It seems counterintuitive, but true comfort in grief is in acknowledging the pain, not in trying to make it go away.

EVERYTHING HAPPENS FOR A REASON

Humans are such funny creatures. We're quick with "comfort," judgment, and meaning-making when it comes to other people's losses. How many times have you heard "Everything happens for a reason" inside your loss? Those same people would be the first to refute that statement if something horrendous happened to them. We use words on one another we would never accept for ourselves.

Things like "Everything happens for a reason" and "You'll become a stronger/kinder/more compassionate person because of this" bring out rage in grieving people. Nothing makes a person angrier than when they know they're being insulted, but they can't figure out how.

It's not just erasing your current pain that makes words of comfort land so badly. There's a hidden subcontext in those statements about becoming better, kinder, and more compassionate because of your loss, that often-used phrase about knowing what's "truly important in life" now that you've learned how quickly life can change.

The unspoken second half of the sentence in this case says you *needed* this somehow. It says that you weren't aware of what was important in life before this happened. It says that you weren't kind, compassionate, or aware enough in your life before this happened. That you needed this experience in order to develop or grow, that you needed this lesson in order to step into your "true path" in life.

As though loss and hardship were the only ways to grow as a human being. As though pain were the only doorway to a better, deeper life, the only way to be truly compassionate and kind.

Statements like this say you were not good enough *before*. You somehow needed this.

It's implied, and certainly the speaker would deny it if you pointed it out. But those ghost words are there. And they matter.

If it were true that intense loss is the only way to make a person more compassionate, only self-absorbed, disconnected, shallow people would experience grief. That would make logical sense. That it doesn't? Well, it proves my point. You didn't need this experience in order to grow. You didn't need the lessons that supposedly only grief can teach. You already were a good and decent human, making your way in the world.

Learning happens in a million different ways. Grief and loss are one path to depth and connection, but they are not the only path. In an essay on post-traumatic growth, a veterans' therapist states that people who look back and see their devastating loss or injury as a growth experience are those who felt most dissatisfied or disconnected in their personal lives before the event. They are not grateful for what happened, but they see the arc of their own development in the shadow of their loss. But for those whose lives were full and deep before their loss? The researcher admits that these participants didn't experience big surges in growth because there were no big surges to make. There's no comfort in "becoming a better person" when you were already happy with the person you were.

Grief is not an enlightenment program for a select few. No one needs intense, life-changing loss to become who they are "meant" to be. The universe is not causal in that way: you need to become something, so life gives you this horrible experience in order to make it happen. On the contrary: life is call-and-response. Things happen, and we absorb and adapt. We respond to what we experience, and that is neither good nor bad. It simply is. The path forward is integration, not betterment.

You didn't *need* this. You don't have to grow from it, and you don't have to put it behind you. Both responses are too narrow and shaming to be of use. Life-changing events do not just slip quietly away, nor are they atonements for past wrongs. They change us. They are part of our foundation as we live forward. What you build atop this loss might be growth. It might be a gesture toward more beauty, more love, more wholeness. But that is due to your choices, your own alignment with who you are and who you want to be. Not because grief is your one-way ticket to becoming a better person.

When you choose to find meaning or growth inside your loss, that's an act of personal sovereignty and self-knowledge. When someone else ascribes growth or meaning to your loss, it diminishes your power, gives subtle shaming or judgment to who you were before, and tells you that you needed this somehow. No wonder it feels so bad.

Words of comfort that imply you needed this, that you needed whatever has happened to rip open your world, can never be of comfort. They're lies. And lies never feel good.

SELF-CHECK AND REALITY CHECKS

There's so much correction inside grief, it can be hard to feel that anything is helpful. For now, it's important to know that most things offered as "support" in our culture are really designed to solve problems or to get you out of pain. If it feels wrong to you, it is. Grief is not a problem to be solved; it's an experience to be carried. The work here is to find—and receive—support and comfort that helps you live with your reality. Companionship, not correction, is the way forward.

The next few chapters further explore the deeper roots of Western culture's inability to be present to pain. While cultural studies may not feel personally relevant, seeing the scope of the problem can help you feel less crazy, less alone, and help you find your own true path inside your loss.

3

IT'S NOT YOU, IT'S US

Our Models of Grief Are Broken

When someone you love has just died, why does it matter that our cultural models of grief are broken? I mean—who cares? This is about you, not everyone else. Except that, especially in early grief, everyone thinks you're doing it wrong. The reflection you get from the outside world can make you think you've gone crazy on top of everything else. The dismissals and platitudes of others can make you feel abandoned inside your grief, just at the moment when you most need to know you're loved.

Your personal experience is affected, intimately, by the wider cultural sweep of grief illiteracy. Seeing that illiteracy laid out can help normalize a wholly abnormal time.

You aren't crazy. The culture is crazy. It's not you; it's us.

> Reexamine all you have been told in school or church
> or in any book, and dismiss whatever insults your
> own soul.
>
> WALT WHITMAN, *Leaves of Grass*

TRICKLE-DOWN PATHOLOGY

Collectively, we wear a massive set of reality blinders when it comes to grief. Clinical counseling training programs devote very little time to the subject, even though most clients will come to us with immense grief. What *is* taught is a hugely outdated system of stages that was never meant to prescribe the correct ways to grieve. What is taught to the medical professions trickles down to the general population.

As a culture, our views on grief are almost entirely negative. Grief is seen as an aberration, a detour from "normal," happy life. Our medical models call it a disorder. We believe that grief is a short-term response to a difficult situation, and as such, should be over and done within a few weeks. Grief that hasn't disappeared, faded back into fond memories and an occasional wistful smile, is evidence that you've done something wrong, or that you aren't as resilient, skilled, or healthy as you thought you were before.

Sadness, grief, pain—they all mean there's something wrong with you. You're stuck in the so-called dark emotions. You aren't following the stages of grief. You're blocking your own recovery, still being so sad. You have a condition now, and it needs to be fixed.

When grief is spoken of in more positive terms, it's always as a means to an end. Our popular psychology, self-help books, movie storylines, book plots, and spiritual texts all glorify grief and loss as a way to grow as a person; to transcend loss is the biggest goal. Happiness is considered the true mark of wellness. Your health and sanity depend on your ability to rise above your grief, to claim equanimity, to find your happiness within.

Your broken heart doesn't stand much of a chance in the face of all this. There's no room for your pain to just *exist*, without pathology.

THE ANTI-GRIEF NARRATIVE AND
THE BIZARRE THINGS WE HEAR

In my own early days, I heard unimaginable things about my grief, about my skills in dealing with grief, and about Matt himself. I was told that I wasn't a very good feminist if I was this upset over "losing a man." I was told that my personal and spiritual development must not have been as good as I thought if I couldn't find the gift in this situation. I also heard that Matt never loved me, that he was happier freed from his body than he ever could have been while alive, that he would be horrified at how badly I was doing. I was told that Matt and I created this, with our intentions. That we had a contract in this life; we agreed to this, and since we agreed, there was no reason to be upset.

I also heard seemingly wonderful things—that I was strong and smart and beautiful, that I would find someone new right away. That I would turn this loss around and make it into a gift, that I should think of all the people I could help. That if I would stop being so sad, I'd feel his love around me (but only if I stopped being so sad). Anything to get me out of my pain and sadness and back into a more acceptable way of being.

The things I was told pale in comparison to stories I've heard from grieving people around the world: You caused your baby's cancer with your unhealed personal issues. You have two other children; you should be thankful they exist. If it was meant to be, she would have lived. It's god's plan. You really need to get over this and move on; they weren't that great of a person anyway. A truly enlightened person is not this attached to the other humans in their life; clearly you're codependent. You must have called this experience to yourself with your thoughts; you needed it for your own learning. So what if you're paralyzed? Some people never get a chance to see what they're really made of, and you do.

Judgment, criticism, and dismissive comments are the norm in deep grief, not the exception. Sure, most people have "good intentions," but the difference between their intentions and the actual impact of their words is vast.

The thing is, people think the whole point of grief is to get out of it as quickly as possible. As if grief were some strange thing, some bizarre, and incorrect, response to someone (or something) you love being torn from your life. Grief gets a narrow window to be expressed. After that, you are expected to return to normal, carrying with you the gifts you've learned from the experience. You're supposed to become wiser, more compassionate, and truly understand what's important. Staying sad means you're not doing it right.

Our cultural ideas are so deeply embedded that it can be hard to describe how it feels to be on the receiving end of what passes for grief support. We'll get into this more deeply in part 3, but it's important to state here that most people simply stop saying how misunderstood they feel in their grief because it seems no one wants to hear it. We stop saying "this hurts" because no one listens.

GETTING STUCK IN GRIEF

I'm often asked what to do when a friend or family member seems to be "stuck" in their grief. My response is always the same: "What would 'not being stuck' look like to you? What are your expectations?" For most people, "not being stuck" means that the person has gone back to work, regained their sense of humor, attends social events, doesn't cry every day, and is able to talk about things other than their loss or their grief. They seem . . . happy again.

We think "happy" is the equivalent of "healthy." As though happiness were the baseline, the norm to which all things settle, when we're living as we should.

In short, "back to normal" is the opposite of "being stuck," and getting back to normal (happy) has to happen fast.

HOW LONG IS TOO LONG?

I remember telling someone I was having a rough day, about five weeks after my partner drowned. "Why? What's going on?" they asked. "Uh. Matt died," I replied. "Still? That's still bothering you?"

Still. Yes. Five days, five weeks, five years. One of the best things someone said to me in the months after Matt died was that, with a loss of this magnitude, "just happened" could mean eight days ago as easily as it meant eighty years. When I speak to someone within the first two years of their loss, I always tell them, "This just happened. It was just a minute ago. Of course it still hurts." Their relief is palpable.

We have it so deeply engrained in us that any kind of hardship shouldn't last more than a couple of months, at most. Anything more than that is considered malingering. As though the loss of someone you love were just a temporary inconvenience, something minor, and surely not something to stay upset over.

Our medical model calls grief that lasts longer than six months a "disorder." Descriptions of so-called complicated grief—grief requiring psychological intervention—include still longing for the person who has died, feelings of injustice, and a pervasive sense that the world can never go back to what it was (and other forms of so-called hopelessness). In real-life experience, that timeline of expectation is actually far shorter. Many clinicians, clergy, and therapists believe that being deeply affected by loss after the first couple of weeks is a faulty response. What the medical model believes moves out to the general population, perpetuating the idea that you should be back to normal as soon as possible.

Medicalizing—and pathologizing—a healthy, normal, sane response to loss is ridiculous, and it does no one any good.

THE STAGES OF GRIEF
AND WHY THERAPISTS FAIL

As a therapist, I often find myself apologizing for my profession. With alarming frequency, I hear horror stories from grieving people who have gone to see therapists for support, only to leave shaken and angry. Grief is routinely dismissed, judged, medicated, and minimized by those in the "helping" professions.

No matter their theoretical orientation to therapy, or their intent to help, clinicians are often the least skilled people in the room. Many grieving people find themselves educating their therapists about the realities of grief.

As I mentioned, our professionals are largely taught the five stages of grief model proposed by Dr. Elisabeth Kübler-Ross in her book *On Death and Dying*, published in 1969. Even if the five stages are not explicitly mentioned, they underlie so much of what counselors and doctors think of as the "healthy" way to grieve. No wonder so many grieving people have given up on getting professional support: the stages don't fit.

The stages of grief were developed by Kübler-Ross as she listened to and observed people living with terminal diagnoses. What began as a way to understand the emotions of the dying became a way to strategize grief. The griever is expected to move through a series of clearly delineated stages: denial, anger, bargaining, and depression, eventually arriving at "acceptance," at which time their "grief work" is complete.

This widespread interpretation of the stages model suggests that there is a right way and a wrong way to grieve, that there is an orderly and predictable pattern that everyone will go through. You must move through these stages completely or you will never heal.

Getting out of grief is the goal. You have to do it correctly, and you have to do it fast. If you don't progress correctly, you are *failing at grief.*

In her later years, Kübler-Ross wrote that she regretted writing the stages the way that she did, that people mistook them as being both linear and universal. The stages of grief were not meant to tell anyone what to feel and when exactly they should feel it. They were not meant to dictate whether you are doing your grief "correctly" or not. Her stages, whether applied to the dying or those left living, were meant to normalize and validate what someone *might* experience in the swirl of insanity that is loss and death and grief. They were meant to give comfort, not create a cage.

Death, and its aftermath, is such a painful and disorienting time. I understand why people—both the griever and those around them, whether personal or professional—want some kind of road map, a clearly delineated set of steps or stages that will guarantee a successful end to the pain of grief.

But you can't force an order on pain. You can't make grief tidy or predictable. Grief is as individual as love: every life, every path, is unique. There is no pattern, and no linear progression. Despite what many "experts" believe, there are no stages of grief.

Despite what the wider population believes, there are no stages of grief.

To do grief well depends solely on individual experience. It means listening to your own reality. It means acknowledging pain and love and loss. It means allowing the truth of these things the space to exist without any artificial tethers or stages or requirements.

You might experience many of the things other grieving people experience, and hearing that can help. But comparing one way of living with loss with another, as though it were a pass-fail endeavor? That is never going to help.

Until our medical professions are taught to come to grief with the respect and care it deserves, it's going to be hard to find therapists who are willing to sit with pain without pathologizing it.

So again, on behalf of my profession, I'm sorry it's so rough out there. There are, in fact, many, many beautifully skilled therapists and doctors. I found them for myself in my own early grief, and I've met many of them as I continue to do this work. If you've looked for professional support and been disappointed, please keep looking. Good people are out there. (And check the resources section at the back of the book for national and regional resources. It's a great place to start.)

> According to some clinical diagnostic criteria, I am suffering from moderate to severe depression, and my anxiety levels are high. My therapist suggests antidepressants and some online cognitive behavioral therapy. I leave feeling worse than when I went in. I'm not just grieving anymore. I'm now mentally ill. Someone in some central NHS office has created a downloadable test that tells me so. It must be true: I am failing grief. I try not to let it get to me, but I wonder again if I should be over this by now. I have passed the six-month milestone after all.
>
> BEVERLY WARD, Writing Your Grief student, on the death of her partner

BUTTERFLIES, RAINBOWS, AND THE CULTURE OF TRANSFORMATION

A lot goes into the making of a grief-illiterate culture. There's so much behind all those simplistic and innocuous-seeming platitudes. We've already talked about the solution-oriented messages behind most of what people say and think about grief, but the roots of our anti-grief culture run deep. The trickle-down effect of the stages of grief model is just the beginning.

Any quick search on the terms "grief" or "hardship" will turn out hundreds of thousands of rainbow-bearing, positive-attitude, "this too shall pass" memes. We acknowledge that hard things happen, sure, but with hard work and the right attitude, everything will turn out great. After all, our movies and books about grief always show the widower, or the grieving mother, coming back even better than before. If things seem a little sad or bittersweet sometimes, it's OK because at least now our hero knows what's really important. That grieving parent created something beautiful out of their child's death, and just think—it wouldn't have happened otherwise. That terrible near-death accident didn't result in death, in fact, it brought the whole family closer together. Things always work out for the best.

Part of our strange cultural relationship with grief comes from a seemingly innocent source: entertainment.

All of our cultural stories are stories of transformation. They're stories of redemption. Books, movies, documentaries, children's stories, even the tales we tell ourselves—they all end on a positive note. We demand a happy ending. If there isn't one, well, that's the hero's fault. Nobody wants to read a book where the main character is still in pain at the end.

We believe in fairy tales and Cinderella stories, stories where, through effort and perseverance, things always work out. We rise to meet adversity head-on. We don't let our troubles get us down, or at least, we don't let them keep us there. Our heroes—whether real or fictional—are models of bravery and courage in the face of pain. The villains, the disappointing characters, are the ones too stubborn to turn their pain around.

We are an overcoming culture. Bad things happen, but we come out better for them. These are the stories we tell. And it's not just on the screen.

Social scientist Brené Brown argues that we live in "a Gilded Age of Failure," where we fetishize recovery stories for their redemptive ending, glossing over the darkness and struggle that precedes it.[1]

We've got a cultural narrative that says bad things happen in order to help you grow, and no matter how bleak it seems, the end result is always worth the struggle. You'll get there, if only you believe. That happy ending is going to be glorious.

Grieving people are met with impatience precisely because they are failing the cultural storyline of overcoming adversity. If you don't "transform," if you don't find something beautiful inside this, you've failed. And if you don't do it quickly, following that narrative arc from incident to transformation within our collective attention span, you're not living the right story.

There's a gag order on telling the truth, in real life and in our fictional accounts. As a culture, we don't want to hear that there are things that can't be fixed. As a culture, we don't want to hear that there is some pain that never gets redeemed. Some things we learn to live with, and that's not the same as everything working out in the end. No matter how many rainbows and butterflies you stick into the narrative, some stories just don't work out.

NARRATIVE RESISTANCE

Without always knowing why, many people rebel against those transformation stories. Or at least, we're beginning to rebel against them. Those easy, tacked-on endings are starting to (very slowly) lose favor.

Honestly, I think this is why the Harry Potter books were so wildly successful. They were dark. J. K. Rowling dove into that darkness, never once making it syrupy or pretty or sweet. Things did not turn out OK in the end, even though there was beauty in the end. Loss, pain, and grief all existed in that world, and they were never redeemed. They were carried.

Rowling's world spoke to us, collectively, because we needed a story that sounded more like us.

Stories are powerful. Throughout human history, mythology, origin stories, and fairy tales gave us images to live into, to pattern our lives after, to learn from. They helped us locate our own experience against the backdrop of something wider. They still do. We still need stories.

We're hungry for a new cultural narrative. One that actually matches the way we live, one that matches the inside of our hearts more than it matches some made-for-TV movie. If we're going to change things, if we're going to create new, valid, realistic, and useful storylines to live into, we have to start by refusing the happy ending. Or maybe, by redefining what a happy ending is.

A happy ending inside grief like yours cannot be a simple "everything worked out for the best." That ending isn't even possible.

THE NEW HERO'S TALE

When Matt died, I went looking for stories of people who had lived this kind of loss. I went looking for stories of people living in pain so huge it obliterated everything else. I needed those stories. An example to live into. What I found were stories of how to get out of pain. How to fix it. How to transform grief as soon as possible. I read over and over that there was something wrong with me for being so upset.

It wasn't just the books that told me that. The people in my life, close friends, the wider community, and the therapists—they all wanted me to be OK. They needed me to be OK because pain like mine, like yours, is incredibly hard to witness. Our stories are very hard to hear.

It wasn't their fault. Not really. They didn't know how to listen. But this is what happens when we only tell stories of how pain can be redeemed: we're left with no stories that tell us how to live in it. We have no stories of how to bear witness. We don't talk about pain that can't be fixed. We're not allowed to talk about it.

We don't need new tools for how to get out of grief. What we need are the skills to withstand it, in ourselves and in others.

Collectively, we carry an immense backlog of grief that has never been heard, simply because we have no story that helps us hear it. We need to tell new stories. We need new stories that tell the truth about pain, about love, about life. We need new stories of bravery in the face of what cannot be fixed. We need to do this for each other; we need to do this *with* each other because pain happens. Grief happens.

If we truly want to be helpful to people in pain, we need to be willing to reject the dominant story of pain as an aberrant condition in need of transformation or redemption. We need to stop trotting out the stages of grief that were never meant to become universal scripts.

In telling better stories, we weave a culture that knows how to bear witness, to simply show up and be present to that which can never be transformed. In telling better stories, we learn to be better companions, to ourselves, and to each other.

Pain is not always redeemed, in the end or otherwise. Being brave—being a hero—is not about overcoming what hurts or turning it into a gift. Being brave is about waking to face each day when you would rather just stop waking up. Being brave is staying present to your own heart when that heart is shattered into a million different pieces and can never be made right. Being brave is standing at the edge of the abyss that just opened in someone's life and not turning away from it, not covering your discomfort with a pithy "think positive" emoticon. Being brave is letting pain unfurl and take up all the space it needs. Being brave is telling *that* story.

It's terrifying. And it's beautiful.

Those are the stories we need.

THERE'S EVEN MORE TO THE STORY . . .

We've covered a lot of cultural territory in this chapter. That wider lens can help you feel more normal, and less crazy, inside your grief. It can also help you as you search for professional and personal support in your grief—identifying those who don't necessarily adhere to the stages model or the cultural narrative of transformation is a great starting point.

If you want to dive even deeper into our collective avoidance of pain and the far-reaching, and surprising, roots of grief shaming, head over to chapter 4. If it feels like too much for right now (early grief really does mess with your ability to take in information), go right to chapter 5. There, you'll find the new vision of grief support and what living your grief well might look like.

4

EMOTIONAL ILLITERACY AND THE CULTURE OF BLAME

There's such a pervasive weirdness in our culture around grief and death. We judge, and we blame, dissect, and minimize. People look for the flaws in what someone did to get to this place: She didn't exercise enough. Didn't take enough vitamins. Took too many. He shouldn't have been walking on that side of the road. They shouldn't have gone to that country if it has a history of monsoons. She shouldn't have gone out to that club, knowing how dangerous it is these days. If he's that upset, he must not have been very stable before this happened. I bet they had unresolved childhood issues—see what unhealed issues do to you?

I have a theory (as yet scientifically unproven) that the more random or out-of-order the loss, the more judgment and correction the grieving person hears. It's like we just can't reconcile the fact that someone could be alive and well at breakfast and dead by lunch. We can't understand how someone who ate well, exercised, and was a generally good human being can get cancer and die at the age of thirty-four. We can't understand how a perfectly healthy child can drop dead of what started as a simple cough. How someone biking to work, using a dedicated bike lane, wearing reflective clothing, their bike adorned with flashing lights, can be struck and killed in an instant.

They had to have done something terribly wrong. There has to be a reason.

It's terrifying to think that someone who seemingly did everything right could still die. It's terrifying to look at a person torn apart by their grief, knowing that could be us someday.

Losses like this highlight the tenuous nature of life. How easily, how quickly life can change.

When Matt died, the one (and only) news story I read blamed him for his death because he wasn't wearing a life jacket. To go swimming. The more polite comments underneath the article made Matt into an angel, looking over everyone, even those who didn't know him; his work on earth was done. Far more of the comments blamed me for "making" him go in the water, or castigated both of us for being too stupid to know better.

In the days after Matt died, I overheard more than one conversation in which people judged my response to Matt's death quite unfavorably. Keep in mind that I wasn't publicly screaming, didn't hit anyone, and wasn't causing big "scenes" anywhere. I was simply—openly—very, very sad.

VICTIM SHAMING AND THE CULTURE OF BLAME

My experience of blame and judgment, both for my grief and of Matt in regard to his own death, is not unique. Most grieving people have felt judged and shamed inside their pain.

Especially when the loss is unusual, violent, or accidental, the backlash of blame is intense: we immediately point out what someone else did wrong. That person did something ridiculous or stupid; we would never do that. It soothes our brains, in some ways, to believe that through our own good sense, we, and all those we love, can be kept safe. And if something bad did happen (through no fault of our own), we'd be strong enough to handle it. Grief wouldn't take us down like that; we'd deal with it so much better than that other person. Everything would be OK.

Brené Brown's research states that blame is a way to discharge pain and discomfort. Intense grief is a reminder that our lives here are tenuous at best. Evidence of someone else's nightmare is proof that we could be next. That's seriously uncomfortable evidence. We have to do some fancy footwork (or rather, fancy brain-work) to minimize our discomfort and maintain our sense of safety.

When someone comes to you in your pain and says, "I can't even imagine," the truth is: they can imagine. Their brains automatically *began* to imagine. As mammals, neurobiologically, we're connected to one another. Empathy is actually a limbic system connection with the other person's pain (or their joy). Being close to someone else's pain makes us feel pain. Our brains know we're connected.

Seeing someone in pain touches off a reaction in us, and that reaction makes us very uncomfortable. Faced with this visceral knowledge that we, too, could be in a similar situation, we shut down our empathy centers. We deny our connection. We shift into judgment and blame.

It's an emotionally protective instinct.

We do this on a personal level, but we also do it globally. We can see this clearly in our cultural epidemics of violence against women and minorities: *the victim must have done something to deserve this.* We see this in our response to large-scale natural and manmade disasters as well: in the aftermath of the 2011 tsunami in Japan, some called it "karmic payback" for Japanese attacks on Pearl Harbor.[1]

In many different ways, in many different forms, our response to others' pain is to lob blame: if something terrible happens, you brought it on yourself.

Blaming someone for their pain—whether that's grief or some kind of interpersonal violence—is our go-to mechanism. How quick we are to demonize rather than empathize. How quick we are to move into debate, rather than hang out in the actual pain of the situation.

At the root of our fears around grief, and in our approaches to grief and loss, is a fear of connection. A fear of acknowledging—really feeling—our relatedness. What happens to one person can happen to anyone. We see ourselves reflected in another person's pain, and we don't like to see ourselves there.

Disasters and deaths bring out a level of emotional empathy that asks you to go there, to acknowledge that this could happen to you or someone you love, no matter how safe you try to be. We hate to see evidence of the fact that there is very little in this life over which we have control. We'll do almost anything to avoid letting that in. What starts as limbic system-based connection reverts to a brain stem survival instinct, an us-or-them response, that puts those in pain on the wrong side of the line, and us, always on the right. We distance ourselves from pain rather than feel annihilated by it.

The culture of blame keeps us safe. Or rather, it lets us believe we're safe.

DOWN THE RABBIT HOLE OF PAIN AVOIDANCE

We want so desperately to see evidence that everyone we love is safe, and will always be safe. We want so desperately to believe we'll survive, no matter what happens. We want to believe we have control. To maintain this belief, we've created—and sustained—an entire culture based on a magical thinking continuum: think the right thoughts, do the right things, be evolved/nonattached/optimistic/faithful enough and everything will be OK. In chapter 3, we talked about the cultural storyline of redemption and transformation. That, too, is part of this survival safety mechanism.

Pain and grief are never seen as healthy responses to loss. They're far too threatening for that. We resist them in equal measure to our fear of being consumed by them.

The problem with this—among many problems—is that it creates a societally acceptable blame structure in which any kind of hardship or pain is met with shame, judgment, and an admonishment to get back to "normal" quickly. If you can't rise above it, you are, once again, doing something wrong.

WHAT ABOUT GOD?

I'd be remiss here if I didn't at least touch on organized religion's part in the culture of pain avoidance. When someone we love is sick or in danger, we pray that they'll be OK. If they survive, we thank god for the escape. "We are so blessed!" is a common way of telegraphing relief in a positive outcome. As we discussed in chapter 2, there's a second half to that sentiment: If god saves some people, especially those who were prayed for, then those who die, or whose outcomes are not what we consider favorable, are therefore . . . not blessed. Prayers, and the humans who prayed them, failed. Either that, or a capricious, all-knowing god had a reason not to save them. This idea that some overarching force of the universe decides who lives and who dies creates, as Cheryl Strayed writes, "a false hierarchy of the blessed and the damned."[2]

In fact, Strayed describes this so perfectly, I can't do it better. In her book *Tiny Beautiful Things*, Strayed addresses a mother wondering what role god might have played in saving her child from a life-threatening illness (or giving it to her in the first place), and if she could still believe in that god had her child died:

Countless people have been devastated for reasons that cannot be explained or justified in spiritual terms. To do as you are asking (why would god do this?) creates a false hierarchy of the blessed and the damned. To use our individual good or bad luck as a litmus test to determine whether or not god exists constructs an illogical dichotomy that reduces our capacity for compassion. It implies a pious quid pro quo that defies history, reality, ethics, and reason.[3]

This belief in a god who can be swayed by human petition is incredibly tricky territory. It's plagued people throughout human history. We can't reconcile our ideas of a loving god—in any tradition—with the horrors that happen on a personal or global scale. What we've created in the face of that cognitive dissonance is the idea that there is a force you can please or displease, through your actions or your petition. It gives us some sense of power and control over what seems to be a random universe full of injustice.

The roots of any tradition call us to love and companion one another inside whatever life brings. Faith is not meant as a means to change the outcome of anything. This vending-machine god who doles out reward and punishment based on our changing ideas of what it means to be "blessed" is a disservice to those who lean on faith in times of hardship. Such a narrow definition of faith is also a disservice to the beautiful traditions we do have: belief in something larger than us helps us survive. It comes up alongside us to help us live what is ours to live but doesn't tell us who is right, who is wrong, who is saved, and who should suffer.

Using faith as a cover for our fears around safety, control, and connection is just one more part of the pervasive culture of blame. It adds an element of spiritual cruelty to an already-challenging path.

THE CULT OF POSITIVITY

It's easier to create sets of rules that let us have the illusion of control than it is to accept that, even when we do everything "right," horrible things can happen. In one form or another, this blame-as-a-form-of-safety idea has been around as long as humans have.

Victim blaming (and grief shaming) is so all-pervasive, we don't always recognize it.

While organized religions have historically trafficked in this model of the one-false-move universe, modern culture has tacked on a New Age, mindfulness-esque yoga-speak around difficulty, death, and grief as well: You create your own reality. Everything that happens on the outside is just a mirror of the inside. You're only as happy as you make yourself be. There's no room for both sadness and gratitude. Intention is everything. Happiness is an inside job. A negative attitude is the only real disability.

Even if we stretch to allow that things happen that are beyond our control, we insist that how we respond *is* in our control. We believe that sadness, anger, and grief are all "dark" emotions, the product of an undeveloped, and certainly less skilled, mind. We might not have been able to prevent what happened, but we can mitigate the effects by simply *deciding* to be all right. Any lasting sign of upset is proof that we aren't seeing this whole thing from the right perspective.

Hidden inside this seemingly encouraging advice to take charge of your emotions, and therefore your life, is that same culture of blame. It's the avoidance of pain clothed in positive, pseudo-spiritual speak. It's the presumption that happiness and contentment are the only true measures of health.

" Over three years now since you left and I am still
tired of having people ask, "How are you?" Do
they really think I will tell the truth? I am tired
of hearing how it was all planned before you were
born and how you and I agreed to your death for
my soul's learning and for yours. No one here
wants to acknowledge that there might just be
chaos and that some things happen because they
can, like cars running people over, like bullets
ripping through a skull or tearing open a heart,
like blood clots filling lungs so you can't get air, or
cancer consuming what is left of the body. A pre-
mapped-out lifetime doesn't make the death of
someone you actually love any less devastating.

I am tired of hearing there is a reason for your
death, for my heartbreak, and that when we get to
the other side it will all make sense. It will never
make sense, even when my heart stops hurting so
much. I miss you. I wish you had never died.

DRU WEST, Writing Your Grief student,
on the death of her daughter, Julia

WHAT'S WRONG WITH BEING POSITIVE?

Author and researcher Barbara Ehrenreich calls this the "tyr-
anny of positive thinking." Her experience with the machinery
of positive thinking (and a forced "happy outlook") came first
from living with cancer, with exhortations to see her diagnosis
as a gift, and to banish "negative" emotions in order to triumph
over her illness:

The first thing I discovered is that not everyone seems
to view this disease with horror or dread. Instead, the

only appropriate attitude is upbeat. This requires the denial of understandable feelings of anger and fear, all of which must be buried under a cosmetic layer of cheer. . . . Without question there is a problem when positive thinking "fails" and the cancer spreads or eludes treatment. Then the patient can only blame herself: she is not being positive enough; possibly it was her negative attitude that brought on the disease in the first place. . . .

[There is] an ideological force in American culture that I had not been aware of before—one that encourages us to deny reality, submit cheerfully to misfortune and blame only ourselves for our fate. . . . In fact, there is no kind of problem or obstacle for which positive thinking or a positive attitude has not been proposed as a cure.[4]

Ehrenreich went on to study positive thinking during the mid-2000s financial crisis, and its ramifications for those who lost their jobs, their homes, and their retirements. Facing poverty and other financial distress, many were told that layoffs and home loss were gifts, and that to be truly successful, one needed to simply believe in oneself and exude a positive attitude. Any external obstacle could be overcome if you believed hard enough. As a way of deflecting responsibility away from the actual corporations that created the collapse, enforced positivity was a brilliant strategy: "What could be a better way of quelling dissent than to tell people who are suffering that it's all their attitude," writes Ehrenreich.[5]

What better way to silence pain than to blame those who feel it?

This kind of blanket rule against complaint, discomfort, or doubt has deep roots. As a way of not addressing the real underlying causes of poverty, violence, inequality, or instability, governments and ruling bodies throughout history have quelled dissent by mandating optimism and by silencing accurate portrayals of the situation. Sharing your doubts or your fears about what was happening could get you killed, or ostracized (which in many cultures meant death, as you were then outside the protection of your community). If enforced optimism didn't work to stem revolt, shifting the focus away from the current reality onto some kind of promised land or heavenly future often did: *The more you suffer now means a greater reward for you later. You're being tested to see how well you can do under pressure.*

We can loop this back to the old religious model on which much of Western culture was built. If something is wrong in your life, it's because you've done something wrong. You've pissed off god (or the ruling class). You weren't following the rules well enough. Suffering is the price of sin. Of course you're being punished. If somehow you were doing everything right, but things still went sideways, well—your reward is in heaven. Those who suffer are closest to god. Your reward is in the afterlife, the promised land, some mythical better time where things work out in the end.

This kind of victim blaming and the glorification of suffering is not new; we just have much prettier language to talk about it now.

Some governments in the world still use blame deflection for political reasons, and it's absolutely present in the way we come to grief and loss in a lot of different cultures. You can see this show up in pop-psychology and New Age renditions of Eastern philosophy, with a slightly different bent: If you're suffering, it's because you aren't in right alignment with your true self. If you were more in touch with your "core," you would have seen this coming. Illness or difficulty is a sign that you were harboring some kind of negativity or resentment—it just showed up in physical form because it was hiding in your thoughts.

Certainly, if something bad does happen, we feel for you. Eastern traditions have taught us that we're meant to have compassion for one another. But everything happens for a reason, and if you were more spiritual, more grounded, more in touch with yourself and with the world, this wouldn't have happened. Maybe you're working out some past karma. Maybe you're storing up good karma for a future self. In some bigger realm, you agreed to this "life lesson." If you really actually were on the path to enlightenment and doing good self-work, and something bad happened anyway, the most enlightened response is to rise above it. Practice nonattachment. Don't let it stress you out. Find the good in it.

Somehow, we are meant to both accept suffering as a gift that we needed in order to become better people *and* refuse to let loss shove us out of our normal, happy, rosy, optimistic demeanor. Painful emotional states aren't meant to last—they're short-term pit stops on the way to a brighter and better (or at least more "normal") *you*. Suffering makes you grow.

It's all part of that cultural storyline that glorifies transformation, while staunchly avoiding the reality of pain in the world.

SPIRITUAL BYPASS AND THE MYTH OF ENLIGHTENMENT

The culture of blame and the epidemic of shutting down grief gets especially convoluted when we look to spiritual, meditative, or other tools of self-reflection and growth.

We've got this idea that being a "spiritual" or "evolved" person means we aren't upset by anything. We hide out in claims to be above pain, or decide we're skilled in Eastern ideas of "nonattachment"; therefore it's unevolved to be upset about anything worldly. Remaining calm and unaffected in any situation is a sign of our spiritual and emotional development.

We've also got this idea that spiritual practices, in and of themselves, are meant to take away our pain, and put us in a place of equanimity. We believe that's what those tools are for: to make us feel better.

No matter how much our culture insists on it, spiritual and meditative practices are not meant to erase pain. That's a symptom of our pain-avoidant culture, and not an accurate portrayal of the practices themselves.

It's a misuse of so many beautiful teachings to force them into roles they were never meant to play.

Spiritual practices in any tradition, including mindfulness in its many forms, are meant to help you live what is yours to live, not make you rise above it. These tools are meant to help you feel companioned inside your grief. They're meant to give you a tiny bit of breathing room inside what is wholly unbearable. That's not at all the same thing as making your pain go away.

Rather than help us rise above being human, teachings in any true tradition help us become *more* human: more connected, not less attached.

So much of what we now call *spiritual bypass* is the age-old split between the head and the heart—trying to surpass being human by becoming more intellectual. We do this because being human *hurts*. It hurts because we love. Because we are connected to those around us, and it's painful when they die. It hurts when we lose what we love. Being a spiritually minded person makes you more open to pain and suffering and hardship—which are all parts of love.

Rising up into our intellectual spheres, trotting out spiritual aphorisms, is just one more way we try to safeguard against *feeling*. It's one more way we try to protect our attachments by denying we have them. We may claim it as higher thinking, but it's our survival instinct brain stem running the show. What we need is our limbic system: our capacity to see ourselves in the other, and respond with love.

The way to get through the pain of being human is not to deny it, but to experience it. To let it exist. To let it be, without stopping it up or holding it back, or in our newer, more modern forms of resistance, by claiming it isn't "evolved" to be in pain. That's garbage. It's elitist. By the same token, you don't "allow" pain so that you can go back to a normative baseline of happiness.

You allow pain because it's real. Because it is easier to allow than to resist. Because being with what is is kinder, softer, gentler, and easier to bear—even when it rips you apart. Because bearing witness to pain, without shutting it down or denying it, *is* enlightenment. Your emotional resilience and intelligence has to be quite secure to be able to hold your gaze on the reality of loss.

Whatever faith or practice you claim, it shouldn't force you to rise above your pain, or deny it somehow. If anything, practice often makes you feel more intensely, not less. When you are broken, the correct response is to be broken. It's a form of spiritual hubris to pretend otherwise.

> Spiritual bypassing—the use of spiritual beliefs to avoid dealing with painful feelings, unresolved wounds, and developmental needs—is so pervasive that it goes largely unnoticed. The spiritual ideals of any tradition, whether Christian commandments or Buddhist precepts, can provide easy justification for practitioners to duck uncomfortable feelings in favor of more seemingly enlightened activity. When split off from fundamental psychological needs, such actions often do much more harm than good.
>
> ROBERT AUGUSTUS MASTERS, *Spiritual Bypassing: When Spirituality Disconnects Us from What Really Matters*

Please know that you are not failing to be a "spiritual" or "emotionally intelligent" person because you are so upset. The fact that you're upset makes perfect sense, and your desire to bear witness to your own pain is a sign of your emotional depth and skill. Empathy—feeling with yourself, feeling with others—is the real hallmark of development.

> I am angry at the Buddhist priest I desperately consulted early on to make myself be "mindful" in my grief. He told me about the Four Noble Truths—that my suffering is all in the mind, and that I needed to let go of my attachment. Those were the cruelest words I ever could hear. He kept saying "it's all in the mind, it's all in the mind." And when I rocked back and forth through my tearstained pain and asked him, "But what about the heart?" he had no answers for me.
>
> MONIKA U. CURLIN, Writing Your Grief student,
> on the accidental death of her husband, Fred

THE COST OF AVOIDING GRIEF

I know all this talk about the historical roots of pain avoidance can make me sound like a cranky curmudgeon, bitching about the state of the world. And in some ways, that is exactly what I am. But here's the thing: I spend all day listening to the pain grieving people carry *on top* of their actual grief. I hear, over and over again, how painful it is to be judged, dismissed, and misunderstood.

The cult of positivity we have does everyone a disservice. It leads us to believe we're more in charge of the world than we are, and holds us responsible for every pain and heartbreak we endure. It sets up a one-false-move world, in which we must be careful not to upset the gods, or karma, or our bodies with our thoughts and intentions. It co-opts tools of comfort and liberation by forcing them into the service of denial and self-deception. It makes us speak useless platitudes to those in grief, harping on some glorious imagined future reward while ignoring their very real and current pain.

How we come to grief is how we come to so much of life. Harvard Medical School psychologist Susan David writes that our cultural dialogue is fundamentally avoidant. As we start to unravel our language around grief and loss, we see how completely true that is—and how many other areas of life it touches.

If we're going to get better at this, if we're going to change things not just for grieving people, but for everyone, we have to talk about the high costs of denying grief in all its forms.

On a personal level, repressing pain and hardship creates an internally unsustainable condition, wherein we must medicate and manage our true sadness and grief in order to maintain an outer semblance of "happiness." We don't lie to ourselves well. Unaddressed and unacknowledged pain doesn't go away. It attempts to be heard in any way it can, often manifesting in substance addiction, anxiety and depression, and social isolation. Unheard pain helps perpetuate cycles of abuse by trapping victims in a pattern of living out or displacing their trauma onto others.

Our foundational inability to tolerate pain, hardship, and horror also keeps us paralyzed in the face of global heartbreak. The amount of pain in the world is staggering, and we work hard not to see it. Our rampant avoidance of feeling-with-each-other requires us to distance ourselves from environmental devastation, from human suffering, from child abuse and sex trafficking, from global wars, from hate crimes of all kinds. When we do see suffering, we throw ourselves into outrage, rather than collapse into grief. Activist and author Joanna Macy speaks of the unrecognized, and unwelcome, pain in the hearts of most activists. It's as if we are afraid the full force of our sadness would render us mute, powerless, and unable to go on. That unacknowledged pain results in burnout, disconnection, and a distinct lack of empathy for others who hold seemingly opposing views.

Our cultural avoidance—and denigration—of our very human losses and pain creates so many problems, it wouldn't be a stretch to say we have an epidemic of unspoken grief.

So while we're largely focused on the broader, cultural refusal of grief as it relates to your personal grief, it's important to recognize how pervasive the problem really is. The gag order on pain is everywhere. Everyone has a role to play in overcoming our pain-averse culture.

> There must be those among whom we can sit down
> and weep, and still be counted as warriors.
>
> ADRIENNE RICH, *Sources*

ATTACHMENT IS SURVIVAL

Pain has to be welcomed and understood, given actual true space at the table; otherwise we cannot do the work we do, whether that is the personal work of showing up and staying alive, or the wider global work of making the world safe, equitable, and beautiful for all beings. We have to be able to say what's true without fear of being seen as weak, damaged, or somehow failing the cultural storyline. We need to make it just as normal to talk about our pain as it is to talk about our joy.

There is no need to rush redemption.

Hard, painful, terrible things happen. That is the nature of being alive, here in this world. Not everything works out;

everything doesn't happen for a reason. The real path here, the real way forward, is not in denying that irredeemable pain exists, but by acknowledging that it does. By becoming a culture strong enough to bear witness to pain, when pain is what is. By sticking together inside what hurts. By opening ourselves to one another's pain, knowing that this, too, could be us the next time around.

When we're afraid of loss, we cling to a system of right and wrong, of well and unwell, to safeguard our connections to those we love. We think barricading ourselves against pain and suffering will help us survive.

Our deeply embedded aversion to pain and hardship—to acknowledging pain and hardship—keeps us from what we most want: safety. Safety in the form of love, connection, and kinship. We defend ourselves against losing it, but in doing so, we keep ourselves from living it.

The tricky thing is, true survival never exists in a world where we have to lie about our own hearts, or pretend we're more in control than we are. It just makes us desperately more anxious and more rabid in our attempts to make everything work out in the end.

The most efficient and effective way to be "safe" in this world is to stop denying that hard and impossible things happen. Telling the truth allows us to connect, to fully enter the experience of another and *feel with them.*

Real safety is in entering each other's pain, recognizing ourselves inside it. As one of my oldest teachers used to say, poignancy is kinship. It's evidence of connection. That we hurt for each other shows our relatedness. Our limbic systems, our hearts, and our bodies are made for this; we long for that connection.

That you see your own potential for grief and loss in someone else's grief? That's beautiful. Poignancy is kinship.

When emotion comes up, we can let that poignancy run through us. It hurts, but it hurts because we're related, because we're connected. It should hurt. There's nothing wrong with that. When we recognize pain and grief as a healthy response to loss, we can respond with skill and grace, rather than blame and bypass. We can respond by loving one another, no matter what happens.

Finding safety means to come together, with open hearts and a willing curiosity about everything we experience: love, joy, optimism, fear, loss, and heartbreak. When there is nothing we can't answer with love and connection, we have a safety that can't be taken away by the external forces of the world. It won't keep us from loss, but it will let us feel held and supported inside what cannot be made right.

The real cutting edge of growth and development is in *hurting with each other*. It's in companionship, not correction. Acknowledgment—being seen and heard and witnessed inside the truth about one's own life—is the only real medicine of grief.

5

THE NEW MODEL OF GRIEF

Having traveled down into the cultural roots of grief avoidance, how do we find our way back out? How do we become, not only people, but a whole wider culture, comfortable bearing the reality that there is pain that can't be fixed? How do we become people who know that grief is best answered with companionship, not correction?

Ignoring, for the moment, this whole wider culture thing, and turning instead to you, inside your own pain, what do you *do* about grief? If no one talks about the reality of living inside unbearable pain, how do you live here at all?

We have to find a new model. A better story to live into.

We've got this idea that there are only two options in grief: you're either going to be stuck in your pain, doomed to spend the rest of your life rocking in a corner in your basement wearing sackcloth, or you're going to triumph over grief, be transformed, and come back even better than you were before.

Just two options. On, off. Eternally broken or completely healed.

It doesn't seem to matter that nothing else in life is like that. Somehow, when it comes to grief, the entire breadth of human experience goes out the window.

There's a whole middle ground between those two extremes (as there is for everything else in life), but we don't know how to talk about it. We don't know how to talk about grief if we step outside that pervasive cultural model of entirely healed or irrevocably broken.

It's such a narrow band of options. I can't work inside that space—it's not real. I don't operate in the transformation model. I can't give a happy ending to things. I can't tie things up in a pretty bow and say, "Everything's going to be OK, and you're going to be even better than before," because I don't believe that and it's not true.

At the same time, I can't leave you with no message to live into. I can't just say, "Sorry, this is going to suck forever and ever, and you'll never feel any different." I can't leave you, or anyone, down in that basement rocking in the corner. That's not appropriate either.

What I'm proposing is a third path. A middle way. Not on, not off. A way to tend to pain and grief by bearing witness. By neither turning away, nor by rushing redemption, but by standing there, right there, inside the obliterated universe. By somehow making a home there. By showing that you can make a life of your own choosing, without having to pick one thing over another: leave your love behind but be "OK," or retain your connections and be "stuck."

Finding that middle ground is the real work of grief—my work, and yours. Each of us, each one of us, has to find our way into that middle ground. A place that doesn't ask us to deny our grief and doesn't doom us forever. A place that honors the full breadth of grief, which is really the full breadth of love.

The only choice we have as we mature is how we inhabit our vulnerability, how we become larger and more courageous and more compassionate through our intimacy with disappearance. Our choice is to inhabit vulnerability as generous citizens of loss, robustly and fully, or conversely, as misers and complainers, reluctant, and fearful, always at the gates of existence, but never bravely and completely attempting to enter, never wanting to risk ourselves, never walking fully through the door.

DAVID WHYTE, *Consolations*

MASTERY VERSUS MYSTERY

There isn't much written on the early parts of grief, that close-to-impact zone where nothing really helps. We're so terrified of intense grief, and the feelings of helplessness it engenders, most resources don't speak to it at all. It's much easier to focus on later grief, months and years down the road, where "rebuilding your life" is a more palatable approach. But early grief is when we most need skill, compassion, and connection. It's where a change in our cultural and personal approaches to grief have the most power and create the most lasting good.

Grief no more needs a solution than love needs a solution. We cannot "triumph" over death, or loss, or grief. They are immovable elements of being alive. If we continue to come at them as though they are problems to be solved, we'll never get solace or comfort in our deepest pain.

In discussing ambiguous loss and the West's foundation of unspoken grief, psychologist Dr. Pauline Boss brings up Western culture's "mastery orientation": we're a culture that loves to solve problems.[1] That mastery orientation is what lets us find cures for diseases, gives us cool technology, and generally makes a lot of life better. The problem with mastery orientation is that it makes us look at everything as a problem to be solved, or a challenge to be vanquished. Things like birth and death, grief and love, don't fit well inside that narrative of mastery.

It's that intention of fixing, of curing, of going back to "normal" that messes with everything. It stops conversation, it stops growth, it stops connection, it stops intimacy. Honestly, if we just changed our orientation to grief as a problem to be solved and instead see it as a mystery to be honored, a lot of our language of support could stay the same.

We can't wage war on the "problem" of grief without waging war on each other's hearts. We need to let what is true be true. We need to find ways to share in the shattering experience of loss—in our own lives and in the larger world. Shoving through what hurts will never get any of us what we most want—to feel heard, companioned, and seen for who we are, where we are.

What we need, moving forward, is to replace that mastery approach to grief with a mystery orientation to love: all the parts of love, especially the difficult ones.

Bowing to the mystery of grief and love is such a different response than fixing it. Coming to your own broken heart with a sense of respect and reverence honors your reality. It gives you space to be exactly as you are, without needing to clean it up or rush through it. Something in you can relax. The unbearable becomes just that much easier to survive.

It seems too intangible to be of use, but finding the middle ground of grief happens only when we turn our gaze to face it directly. When we allow the reality of grief to exist, we can focus on helping ourselves—and one another—survive inside pain.

A BETTER WORLD

The new model of grief is not in cleaning it up and making it go away; it's in finding new and beautiful ways to inhabit what hurts. It's in finding the depth of love necessary to witness each other's pain without rushing in to clean it up. It's in standing beside each other, offering companionship.

Changing the way we come to pain creates a new world, one based on sovereignty and kinship, on poignancy and grace. When we stop resisting that which hurts, we're freed to make real changes, changes that help us align with a world where suffering is reduced and love is our primary medicine.

That new model of grief allows us to bring compassion to ourselves and to others. It lets us join each other in all parts of life. It calls us into our best, deepest selves.

I can make it sound so poetic, but the truth is—who knows what kind of world we might create when we turn to fully face all the ways our hearts get broken? What things might change? What kind of world might we create? When the full expression of what it means to love—which includes losing that which we love—is given room to unfold?

We can never change the reality of pain. But we can reduce so much suffering when we allow each other to speak what is true, without putting a gag order on our hearts. We can stop hiding from ourselves, and hiding from each other, in some misguided attempt to be "safe." We can stop hiding what it is to be human. We can craft a world where you can say, "This hurts," and have those words simply received, without judgment or defense. We can clean out the backlog of pain that keeps us trapped in shallow relationships and cycles of disconnection. We can stop making the other "other," and instead protect and support each other as family.

It won't be a world with less grief. But it will be a world with so much more beauty.

Self-compassion is approaching ourselves, our inner experience with spaciousness, with the quality of allowing which has a quality of gentleness. Instead of

our usual tendency to want to get over something, to
fix it, to make it go away, the path of compassion is
totally different. Compassion allows.

ROBERT GONZALES, *Reflections on Living Compassion*

THE PERSONAL IS GLOBAL;
THE GLOBAL IS PERSONAL

The more we speak of the reality of grief, the easier it becomes. The
more people tell the truth about how hard this is—how hard it
is to be alive, to love, and to lose—the better this life becomes
for everyone. Even for those who think that grief is a problem
to be solved.

Our friends, our families, our books, our cultural responses,
are most useful, most loving and kind, when they help those
in grief to carry their reality, and least helpful when they try to
solve what can't be fixed.

Our approaches to ourselves, in our own grief, are most
useful, most loving and kind, when we find ways to keep our
hearts open in the midst of the nightmare, to not lose sight of
love amidst the wreckage.

If we're going to live here, if we're going to get through this
together, if we're going to "get through it" at all, we need to
start being more comfortable with pain. We have to let it go all
the way through us, without looking for reasons or outcomes
or placing blame. We have to stop other-izing one another as a
ward against loss. We have to let the knowledge of our tenuous,
fleeting, beautiful existence be a real part of our lives, not some
story that only happens to other people.

We have to find ways to show our grief to others, in ways
that honor the truth of our own experience. We have to be
willing to stop diminishing our own pain so that others can
be comfortable around us.

Things can be made tangibly different for people in pain—we can change things. We can love each other, standing in the full knowledge that what we love will die. We can love each other, knowing that feeling the other person's pain is a sign of our connection, not our doom. It's terrifying to love one another this way, but it's the way we need to love. Our own personal lives and our larger, global, interconnected lives call us to love in this way. The middle ground of grief, the new model of grief, allows us to love each other that way. It's the only way forward.

BACK TO YOU . . .

We're creating the new model of grief, right now, with these words. I know you didn't mean to be part of the revolution. I know you'd gladly give all this up just to have your old life back. It isn't a fair trade. And we need you. We need you to claim your right to be supported in ways that honor the person you are, the person you were, and the person this loss will have you become. Finding your own middle way helps you, and helps all those who enter the world of grief behind you.

Discussions about the culture of grief are important. It helps to locate yourself inside the larger sweep of cultural emotional illiteracy. It helps knowing you aren't crazy, you aren't wrong, and you aren't broken. The culture is broken, but you? You're fine. That you're in pain doesn't change that fact.

Continuing to show up, continuing to look for support inside your pain, when all the world tries to tell you it's a problem, is an act of fierce self-love and tenacity. Grief is not a sign that you're unwell or unevolved. It's a sign that love has been part of your life, and that you want love to continue, even here.

You are here now, and here sucks.

There aren't a lot of tools for early grief, but there are tools. There are ways to come to yourself with kindness, to build on what you already know of yourself, to help you survive.

My hope is that the tools and practices in this book help you map your own third way, find your own middle ground, neither hopelessly doomed nor forced into a faux positivity that asks you to abandon your own heart.

I don't mean for this book to remove your pain. In telling the truth about grief, I want you to see your own pain reflected back to you. I want you to feel, in the reading, that you have been heard.

As the poet and activist Joanna Macy writes, that your world is in pain is no reason to turn your back on it. The next part of this book leaves the wider culture and returns to your personal grief. May the words you find there help you stay close to your heart, and carve your own path in the wilderness.

PART II

WHAT TO DO WITH YOUR GRIEF

ON RIGHT TIMING: A NOTE
BEFORE WE GET STARTED

I devoured books on grief and loss when Matt first died. I hated most of them. I would flip to the back of a new book to see if the widowed author had remarried. If they had, I wouldn't read the book—clearly, they did not understand what it was like to be me. I would get all excited reading the first few chapters of a new book on loss, only to hurl it away in disgust when subsequent chapters started talking about rebuilding my life and all the great things I might do as a result of this loss.

The problem wasn't always in the books themselves. There are plenty of good books out there. The problem was that most of those books spoke to later grief. They spoke to a time when the world had stopped tilting so violently, when all the dust had settled, and the immediacy of grief was not so sharp. That's a great time to talk about rebuilding—or building—a new life. But when your life has newly exploded? That is not the time for books on how to build a great and glorious future.

So there's something important here about right timing: thoughts about how you'll live inside this grief need to match what you are currently living. If something (even in this very book) feels offensive to you, it's probably not a good match for where you are: there's a timing mismatch. In the early days, survival is different from survival over the weeks, months, and years to come. As you're looking for things to help you survive your loss, you might ask yourself what you most need, and look for those resources that can speak to that place.

What I've outlined in this book is not about fixing your grief, nor is it about the future that awaits. It's meant to help you survive—right here, right now. May you find something useful in these words.

6

LIVING IN THE
REALITY OF LOSS

The only way I know to start talking about the reality of grief is to begin with annihilation: there is a quiet, a stillness, that pervades everything in early grief. Loss stuns us into a place beyond any language. No matter how carefully I craft my words, I cannot reach where this lives in you. Language is a cover for that annihilated stillness, and a poor one at that.

But words are all we have, all I have, to reach you in this place. Please know that I'm aware of how impossible this is, how none of my words will really change anything.

Acknowledgment is one of the few things that actually helps. What you're living can't be fixed. It can't be made better. There are no solutions. That means that our course of action inside grief is simple: helping you gauge what's "normal" and finding ways to support your devastated heart. This part of the book is about helping you survive the bizarre territory of intense grief.

Naming the craziness of this time is powerful: it helps to know what's normal when nothing *feels* normal.

In this chapter's short sections, we cover some of the most common questions, concerns, and challenges inside grief. It's a bit of a crazy quilt, jumping from one weirdness to the next, but there's just so much to juggle inside grief—it really is all over the place. When there's a tool to use to manage the crazy, I've included it. Where there is no tool, acknowledgment is the best medicine.

I haven't addressed all the challenges of grief, or the questions about what's normal: there are simply too many. If there's something you want answered, please be in touch.

> You would say—why do people need to keep ashes? Can't they just let go? Yes. Yes, babe. Eventually, I will take those bones and those teeth and that body I love to the river and to the woods. I will release that vessel I've loved so much, in so many different ways. But right now, your remains remain—safely sealed in a plastic urn inside a plastic bag inside a cardboard box sealed with tape and a sticker bearing your name. To take them out is to see you, to see the body I have loved, reduced to a permanent state of ash. Right now, I can't let go. I can't let this in. I can't accept this in any way. I cannot swallow this truth, that you are gone, that the life we planned is done. If I try to look directly at that fact (that I refuse to let be fact), I feel the explosion start inside of me, the world cracks and my lungs fill, and I cannot breathe. All I know is that I cannot do that. I cannot look directly at this. Everything inside me will explode, and I cannot bear the tearing. It's too big. It's too severe. I'm being beaten by all this—the packing and the moving, your truck in my driveway that will be sold in the next two days, the bed in pieces in my room, waiting to be rebuilt, your photos, your ashes, the people

clamoring for pieces of you, all of our things piled in various rooms. You are gone, and I can't know that now. That you were here, that moment, just a regular moment, and then you were gone.

From my early journals

FOR ALL YOU'VE HAD TO DO . . .

The sheer number of things you need to do when someone has died is mind-boggling. Somehow, things get done. You sit down with your kids, or your partner, or your parents and say the words you should never have to say. You call everyone on the phone list: reciting the facts over and over again, simple, direct. You talk with reporters and doctors and search teams. You shop for the best price on cremation or burial. Call landlords, organize memorials, locate someone to take care of the dog. Eulogies are written, or quiet, personal prayers are said.

There isn't enough paper in the world to write down all the minute details that death brings into your life. Again, I circle back to acknowledgment as the only form of medicine that helps: for everything you've had to do, love—I'm so sorry.

It's OK to let people help where they can, if that relieves some of your burden. For some people, taking care of these details is the last tangible, intimate act of love they can do for the person who's died. There's no one right answer. Delegate what feels overwhelming, and wherever possible, don't let anyone take over acts of intimacy that feel important to you.

 Everything is over.

It was probably my mom who answered the phone. She would have screamed when she heard the news. My dad would have come running from another room, and my god he would have seen her crying, and then she had to tell him, she had to open her mouth and say the words even when she didn't understand them. They are in pain, because this hurts them, but they are somehow going to ask the woman on the phone to tell them where I am. And my god, they are going to want to protect me, and my god it's going to torment them that they can't, but my god they are going to get me on the phone anyway in spite of all of this to tell me that they love me and to tell me that they are getting in the car and that they are coming, they are coming, they are coming, they are telling my brother, and they are all coming three hours to be with me now.

Later that night back in the hospital, when I could breathe enough to speak again, I fumbled for my phone and began the long process of letting people know that she had died. She was extremely popular and loved by a sprawling and complex network of friends. There were so many calls to be made, each one setting off a new shock wave.

ERIC W, widowed at age thirty-seven,
writing on the accidental death of his fiancée, Lisa

TELLING THE STORY

You might find that you tell the story of your loss again and again, even (or especially) to random strangers, or people you've just met. Or, in your mind, you rehearse the events that led up to this loss again and again.

That's all normal. Humans are storytelling creatures: it's why we have cultural mythologies, creation stories, and movies. Telling the story of this loss over and over—it's like we're looking for an alternate ending. A loophole. Some way the outcome might have changed. Could still change. Maybe we missed something. If we can only get the story right, none of this would be happening.

It doesn't matter that that's not "logical." Logic means nothing.

Telling the story feels both necessary and torturous. It *is* both necessary and torturous. We'll talk about this more in the section on grief and anxiety, but for now, please know that this is a normal part of grief. Repetition of the story is a safety mechanism, one way the creative mind tries to reorder the world when it's been dissolved. We tell the story again and again because the story *needs* to be told—we're looking for some way this makes sense, even if it never can.

If you can't tell your story to another human, find another way: journal, paint, make your grief into a graphic novel with a very dark storyline. Or go out to the woods and tell the trees. It is an immense relief to be able to tell your story without someone trying to fix it. The trees will not ask, "How are you *really*?" and the wind doesn't care if you cry.

LITTLE LAND MINES

How many times have people encouraged you to take your mind off this for a while, or they've avoided speaking your person's name so they don't "remind" you of what you've lost? As if you could forget, even for a moment.

We all need a little respite. You can't keep staring at loss every single second; your physical organism simply can't withstand it. The tricky thing is, especially in early grief, pain is everywhere. There is nothing that isn't connected to loss. Taking a break from pain often backfires miserably.

Going to the movies can be an especially cruel experience: you go for a non-sad movie, only to find the main character is widowed, or you realize, halfway through, that you can never crack jokes with your sister about this movie, or that your child will never see it.

Innocuous, everyday things become loaded: The first time you have to fill out a form and choose "widowed," or you're asked how many children you have. When you get to the "emergency contact" part of a form, and realize you can no longer put down the name of the person who has held that spot for years. Dragging yourself to a party, thinking you need to get out more, only to have every single small-talk question point to only one answer: death.

And it's not just when you go looking for distraction: everyday life is full of reminders and grief land mines that the non-grieving wouldn't even think of. When someone you love dies, you don't just lose them in the present or in the past. You lose the future you should have had, and might have had, with them. They are missing from all the life that was to be. Seeing other people get married, have kids, travel—all the things you expected out of life with your person—gone. Seeing other children go to kindergarten, or graduate, or get married—all those things your child should have done, had they lived. Your kids never get to know their brilliant uncle; your friend never gets to read your finished book. Whatever the relationship, seeing evidence of those same relationships going on in the rest of the world is brutal, and unfair, and impossible to withstand.

Especially in the early days, the effort to join the world again is Herculean and monumental. Those densely scattered grief land mines are hard to face. Human interaction is often exhausting. Many people choose to shrink their world down considerably, refusing invitations to anything and everything. Even staunch extroverts find that they need a lot more time alone and quiet than they ever did before.

Please know that if the outside world feels too harsh or too saturated with all things grief, you aren't being "too sensitive." The world *is* full of things connected to your grief. If there is anything that gives you even a moment's relief or respite, move toward that. It makes no difference what it is. Finding a break in grief is nearly impossible, but those occasional breaks are necessary. A day (or more) inside a blanket fort of your own choosing is healthy.

GRIEF AT THE GROCERY STORE

It comes up often enough as a stressor that one task of every-day life needs to be addressed on its own: the grocery store. In early grief, a "simple" trip to the grocery store is anything but simple—you could run in to any number of people who want to know, "How are you *really*?"

Those well-meaning, yet intrusive, questions into your inner emotional state can come at any time, no matter how much you may not want to talk about it.

It's funny, whenever I talk about the specific difficulties of grocery shopping, almost everyone has their own story to share—some shop only after 10:00 p.m. to avoid any people they might know; others drive an hour out of their way just to be able to shop anonymously.

That's yet another thing people outside grief wouldn't normally think about: how, especially if your loss was out of order or unusual, it becomes a topic up for public discussion. Anytime you are out in public, people feel the need to come close, to ask, to check on you. It doesn't often matter whether you are friends with the person or not. In fact, the more distant the relationship, the more probing you might receive while hovering over the produce bin.

I know I stopped shopping at a certain store because a friend of a friend worked there; if she saw me, a long, drawn-out inquiry would begin, with questions about my emotional health, my plans for the future, and requests for intimate details about what actually happened at the river that day. I realize I could have told her to stop, but that took energy, interest, and skills I did not have in me at that time. Shopping somewhere else made more sense.

No wonder grief is so exhausting. It's not *just* the intense actual pain of loss. It's the sheer number of tiny things that need to be avoided, endured, planned for. Impossible to tell from the outside, but those of us in grief absolutely understand. We all have our stories of exhaustion, avoidance, and the need to just not talk.

It's OK to avoid people. It's OK—even healthy—to drive an hour out of your way just to get groceries in order to buy yourself some anonymity. You deserve that distance. You deserve the right to tell your stories when and where you see fit, with a vast, invisible shield of protection for you, as you move in the world without wanting to talk to anyone at all.

Whatever you need in order to feel that protection, that's the thing to do.

And one more thing about the grocery store: many people get overwhelmed with all the things they no longer need to buy for the person they lost—there is no need for their favorite cookies or their morning tea. Abandoned shopping carts are quite common in the world of grieving hearts. Other than home grocery delivery (a great thing, by the way), there's really no way around that one. Rules around self-kindness apply here: pace yourself, allow yourself to leave the store when you need to (no matter how full your cart is), and give yourself some time after the trip to breathe into how hard this all is. "Normal" life tasks often bring your loss into the sharpest contrast.

WHEN IS IT TIME TO . . .

Because there's so much unsolicited advice and opinion floating around the grief world, it's easy to lose track of what you actually want for yourself. Many people write to me wondering when is the "right time" to remove their wedding rings, or convert their child's bedroom into a guest room, or stop referring to their brother in the present tense.

The answer is simple: there is no right time.

You can't wait for the time to feel right, because it likely never will. None of this is something you would ever *choose*. When you're trying to make a decision, you can't wait until it feels *good*.

I like the vomit metric for making decisions: If taking off your wedding rings makes you feel sick, it's not the right time to take them off. If you start to panic at the thought of moving anything in your child's room, then don't move anything. If someone has told you it's time to donate your sister's clothes and you break out in hives, immortalize her closet.

You don't have to change anything until you're ready. There are weird family politics to contend with at times for sure, but for the most part, what you do with things in your home or on your body is up to you. When you make larger life decisions—like when (or whether) to date, sell your house, or change careers—is entirely up to you. No time is the right time. Nothing is too early or too late.

Along these same lines, it's perfectly normal to leave things exactly as your person left them. Evidence that they were here, that they lived, that they were part of you is important. When your life has evaporated, those touchstones become the whole world.

A friend whose husband drowned the year after Matt died told me she kept a bottle of his hot sauce with her through two different moves. She couldn't bear to see the refrigerator without it, even though she would never open the bottle again. I kept the container of ice cream Matt and I bought two nights before he died right up until I moved across the country—four years later.

It was nearly a year before I changed the sheets on the bed where we last slept.

You will do what you need to do when you need to do it. Not a moment before. It will never feel *good*. But if it makes you feel sick, now is not the time. Use the vomit metric for any decisions you have to make and for the ones you feel like you're *supposed* to make.

ON ANNIVERSARIES AND MEMORIALS

What do we do on his death date? Am I supposed to celebrate our wedding anniversary, or their birthday, even when they're dead? Do they have birthdays when they're dead?

Both my mother and my mother-in-law wanted me to be excited about, and involved in, their projects to memorialize Matt's life, an excitement I did not have in me at that time. Every time they went on about this tree or that garden, and how I needed to be involved, or choose, or attend, I had to fight back the words: "I don't want a stupid tree. I want him back!" "I don't care what kind of flowers you put there; it's your garden, not his." And, oh, the number of times I had to bite my tongue and use my grown-up words when some distant family member insisted on a hyperreligious memorial that would have made even Matt lose his temper.

In the end, of course, no one could truly win: no matter what got planted or who gathered in his name, my love was still dead. He was still not coming back.

There is no one right way to honor someone you love. Each relationship leaves its mark; each mark is yours alone. Your way of memorializing a life is right *only* for you.

One of the best things someone said to me as I approached Matt's one-year date was, "You always have the right to leave, even if you just got there, even if you planned the whole thing. No one else has to live this like you do. Leave whenever you need." Just having that permission to leave made it easier to stay.

No matter what you've planned, you can change your mind at any time. It's also OK to not plan anything, instead waiting to check in with yourself when that special date comes. Often, the lead-up to a big date is harder than the date itself. Maybe you want to do something, maybe not.

You might ask other family members and friends how they'd like to plan the day. Encouraging conversation, leaving room for resistance and refusal, is an elegant way to gauge how the people in your life are feeling about these dates. For your own close family unit (or, to be blunt, what is left of it), incorporate elements of each person's vision into the day.

While others may join in your plans, remember that they will have their own expressions, too. They deserve the right to decline, to pull away, to not participate. Everyone grieves differently, and everyone has a different way they memorialize or acknowledge the person who is gone. To the best of your ability, offer respect to other ways of doing this, while honoring your own needs.

Remember that no one is likely to be 100 percent happy. In fact, memorials and anniversary events are often a hot spot: tempers flare, old issues resurface, social skills erode. Whatever you choose to do, or not do, do your best to pace yourself. Keep checking in with your heart about what you might need in any given moment. None of this is easy, even if what you've planned goes beautifully.

KIDS AND GRIEF

It might also be true for you that it's not just yourself you need to think about. No matter what their ages, your children will be affected by grief—whether it's their loss directly, or they're living with the effects of grief on you.

My stepson turned eighteen the day after his father died. Not super young, but in many ways still a child. The outside world saw him as an adult that day. He was called to make decisions no child should have to make.

He'd always been rather quiet about his own internal feelings, and living through his grief was no exception. In the weeks and months that followed, we talked *around* what had happened. We talked about the inner world of grief, and how different people process it differently. His tendency to be more private, plus his natural teenager-ness, meant he didn't say very much about his dad. He said even less about himself.

Given that my stepson was older, and struck out on his own soon after Matt died, I didn't have the same worries that many of you have as you parent your children through loss. I didn't have the heartbreak of seeing a very young child grow up with few to no physical memories. I didn't worry about how other kids would treat my stepson at school, or how the teachers would handle his loss. I worry about his life unfolding without his father's guidance, but I know he had eighteen years of soaking in his dad's presence and influence. I can only hope his father's love infuses him, holds him up, helps him—even now.

Someone asked me the other day if I thought my stepson had "processed" his dad's death, or if it continues to affect him. How can it not continue to affect him? His dad is still dead.

I think we're always looking for evidence that our kids are OK. So much of any emotional process is on the inside. A loss like this will grow and change inside our kids' hearts, changing not just with the passage of time, but also with their changing capacity to absorb and respond to their parent's, or a sibling's, death.

I think all we can do, all any of us can do, is continue to be open about pain, death, grief, and love in age-appropriate ways. We can let our kids know that they can ask us anything. We can let them see our own grief in a way that says, "This hurts, and it's OK to feel it." We can ask, knowing that they may not be willing—or able—to voice what they feel.

Sometimes it takes a lifetime to be able to say what you've lost, to see the many ways a family member's death shaped and changed you. I hope for my kid, and for yours, that our love stays beside them. That the love of the one they've lost stays with them. That they learn to tolerate their own pain, open their heart, and listen for their own voice. Even if they never tell us a word.

Note: Given that I did not have young children at home, I'm not an expert in the effect of loss on kids. The best place I know for resources on how to help grieving kids—in fact, whole grieving families—is the Dougy Center in Oregon. Though their headquarters are in Portland, they are an international agency, and they can point you in the right direction as you navigate loss inside your family.

SPEAKING OF FAMILY . . .

Sometimes families really do stick together and cooperate after a death or catastrophic event. Those are the exceptions, not the rule. Nothing brings out the crazy in a family quite like death.

Arguments over what is done with the body (especially if there was no legal document outlining the person's wishes), whether or not there should be a permanent memorial, what anniversary events should look like—in the best of worlds, these things would be negotiated with skill, compassion, and understanding. The best of worlds, however, doesn't often exist.

Death throws a monkey wrench into family dynamics. Strained relationships that had found a relatively happy level of mutual tolerance flare into knockdown fights. Opinions and needs all jockey for space; everyone needs to be seen and be heard. Old conflicts get brought up. Relatives who were distant in life come out of the woodwork; people you think have your back disappear into their own wounded silence.

Death shakes everyone up.

In my own experience, and in the stories I've heard, it seems that however someone behaved pre-death, they will be more of that in the aftermath of death. The people who tend to be calm and rational remain calm and rational. Those who try to include varying viewpoints, coming to an argument with compassion and patience, tend to do more of the same. And those who argue, blame, and generally act with poor skills . . . do that.

There are so many different ways family conflict shows up in these situations; I can't cover all of them. Maybe what's more effective than coming up with a solution for each scenario is to give you one way to respond to all of them. In all interpersonal challenges—death related or otherwise—my usual advice is to behave in such a way that you can look back on the experience and feel you used good, healthy skills of negotiation, compassion, and self-advocacy. The way you behave under this kind of stress is really the only thing under your control.

■ ■ ■

If you've found yourself arguing over what goes where and how, please be gentle with each other's hearts—including your own. There's really no winner in these situations. No matter who wins the battle over memorials or possessions, the person you love is still dead.

This really is a time to ask yourself which of these battles feels most important to you, and place your energy there. It's not necessary—or helpful—to fight every battle, or respond to every challenge. Sometimes ignoring poor behavior or bratty demands is the wisest action. Do your best to maintain healthy boundaries, voice your needs, and step away from battles when you can. If something is important to you, advocate for yourself and your family, and remember that no matter what the outcome, your love and connection to the person you've lost can never be taken away.

HAS GRIEF ENDED YOUR FRIENDSHIPS?

Normally, when dealing with intense family dynamics, I'd encourage you to lean on your sane, dependable friends for a reality check about the way healthy people interact. My hope is that you have at least a few of those beautiful people in your life.

And—it's one of the cruelest aspects of intense loss: at a time when you most need love and support, some friends either behave horribly or they disappear altogether. There are disappointments and disagreements. Old grudges resurface. Small fault lines become impassable distances. People say the weirdest, most dismissive and bizarre things.

Grief changes your friendships. For many, many people, it ends them. We'll talk more about this in part 3, but for now, I'd be remiss if I didn't mention how common, and how painful, this aspect of grief can be. Your loss intersects with often hidden or especially painful heartbreak in the people around you. Your pain bumps up against their pain. We may not call it that directly, but that's often what's happening when people behave poorly or fail to understand the immensity of your loss. And even when your friends want to support you, we don't often have the skills—no matter how skilled we truly are—to witness and withstand another's pain. Feeling helpless in the face of loss makes people do strange things.

No matter what the deeper reasons are, the loss of friends you thought would stand by you through thick and thin is an added heartbreak. The injustice of these second losses makes grief itself that much more difficult.

THE ONE THING PEOPLE REALLY
DON'T LIKE TO TALK ABOUT: RAGE

I can't end this chapter without talking about anger and rage. There are a million other things that belong in this chapter, and there simply isn't room. But anger? It deserves a place here. The reality of anger never gets any positive airtime in our culture. You're not supposed to be angry. No matter what's happened, showing anger is . . . unseemly. Much like grief, anger is met with deep discomfort: it's fine in short doses, but it needs to be moved through quickly, without much noise.

This boycott on anger is ridiculous.

All emotion is a response to *something*. Anger is a response to a sense of injustice. Of course you're angry: whatever has happened to you is unjust. It doesn't matter whether "fairness" is logical, or whether there's a reason something happened.

Contrary to pop-psychology and the medical model, anger is healthy, normal, and necessary. As with most things, if it isn't given recognition and support, it gets turned inward, where it can become poisonous. What we don't listen to (or refuse to listen to) doesn't go away—it just finds other ways to speak. Shushed anger joins a backlog of disallowed emotion, popping up in health issues, interpersonal challenges, and mental torment. Those negative images we have of rage actually come from anger that isn't allowed to exist: repression creates pressure, which creates toxic behaviors set atop what used to be a healthy response to injustice.

Anger, allowed expression, is simply energy. It's a response. Allowed expression, it becomes a fierce protective love—for yourself, for the one you've lost, and in some cases, gives you the energy to face what is yours to face. Shown respect and given room, anger tells a story of love and connection and longing for what is lost. There is nothing wrong with that.

All of this is to say that your anger surrounding your loss is welcome. It's healthy. It's not something to rush through so you can be more "evolved" or acceptable to the people around you. Find ways to give your sense of injustice and anger a voice. When you can say you're angry, without someone trying to clean it up or rush you through it, it doesn't have to twist back in on itself.

Touching your anger can be scary. If it feels too big, lean on a trusted friend or therapist. This is one place having an ally is really useful. It's OK to ask people how they feel about hearing your anger—it lets them be prepared to really listen, and allows you to know whether they can hear what's true without trying to rush you through your anger before it's had its say.

AND EVERYTHING ELSE?

This chapter is meant to give you a sense of normalcy inside a wholly abnormal time. I can't possibly touch on everything here, but the underlying reality of anything you're facing in your grief is that everything is . . . normal. Acknowledgment of your reality is powerful medicine. It's often the only thing that helps.

The following chapters go into more detail about specific challenges inside grief—the places where there are concrete tools to help manage what can never actually be fixed.[1]

7

YOU CAN'T SOLVE GRIEF, BUT YOU DON'T HAVE TO SUFFER

Living inside grief, you know there is nothing to be fixed: this can't be made right. While most grief support (and well-meaning friends and family) encourages you to move through the pain, that's simply the wrong approach.

The way to live inside of grief is not by removing pain, but by doing what we can to reduce suffering. Knowing the difference between pain and suffering can help you understand what things *can* be changed and what things simply need your love and attention.

Being allowed to tend to your grief, without feeling like you need to fix it or clean it up, makes grief, itself, easier. Reducing suffering while honoring and supporting pain is the core of this book and the focus of this chapter.

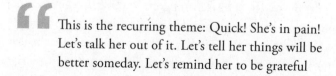 This is the recurring theme: Quick! She's in pain! Let's talk her out of it. Let's tell her things will be better someday. Let's remind her to be grateful

for what she had. Let's tell her how smart and funny and kind she is. And let's be sure, because we know it's weighing her down, to reassure her that someone other than the man she loves will eventually be beside her, snoring softly, waking up to kiss her good morning, rolling back over to have five more minutes while she gets up to walk the dog so he can sleep. Great. Bring it on. Thanks so much for your kind words. You've really relieved my suffering, with all this trying to talk me out of it.

The people I love, the ones I will go to again and again, are the ones who do not in any way try to "solve" this for me, or fix it, or fix me. They do not make any attempt to cheer me up, or shame me into feeling thankful that I had as much love as I did, and so should be happy with that. They do not tell me things will be better "later," and that I have so much to live for. They do not remind me I am part of the cycle of life. As though that matters, all that pandering, condescending crap.

Excerpted from "Ask, Don't Tell: How to Help Someone in Grief" on refugeingrief.com

WHAT DO I DO NOW?

The first weeks and months after an out-of-order death are a world unto themselves. At that initial time of impact, few things bring comfort. Things that brought comfort in the past become flimsy under the weight of this kind of grief. Words of intended comfort just grate. Encouragement is not helpful. Platitudes never help.

Survival in early grief has a very small circumference. It's not an ordinary time, and ordinary rules do not apply. In grief, especially early grief, you have little energy to use any "tools" whatsoever. And tools used in the service of making things *better* often feel more offensive than helpful.

Platitudes, "self-help," well-meaning advice, and suggestions—they're *all* about getting you out of pain. Whenever we talk about how much we hurt, someone is right there to help make that pain go away. In this model, pain is a bad thing, and it must be removed. But your pain is valid. It won't just go away.

In his book *The Body Keeps the Score*, Bessel van der Kolk writes that the body needs to express itself when exposed to stimuli. It *has* to. It needs to. When the body and mind experience pain, we have a biological need to express it. Pain that is not allowed to be spoken or expressed turns in on itself, and creates more problems.

Unacknowledged and unheard pain doesn't go away. One of the reasons our culture is so messed up around grief is that we've tried to erase pain before it's had its say. We've got an emotional backlog sitting in our hearts.

You can't heal someone's pain by trying to take it away from them. You can't gloss over pain as though it were in the way of some "better" life. That grief is painful doesn't make it wrong. Pain is a normal and healthy response to loss. The way to survive grief is by allowing pain to exist, not in trying to cover it up or rush through it.

Rather than erase pain, we might tend to it as though it were healthy and normal, in need of our kind, compassionate, simple honesty and care. We might, instead, companion ourselves inside pain. Only in tending to it can we bear what is unbearable.

PAIN VERSUS SUFFERING: ONE GETS TENDED; ONE GETS "FIXED"

And this is where we come up against our need to fix things, our need to take positive action on our own behalf. If we don't "fix" pain, if we don't solve grief, are we just doomed to relentless torture for the foreseeable future?

For our purposes here, it's useful to separate pain and suffering. Pain is pure and needs support rather than solutions, but suffering is different. Suffering *can* be fixed, or at least significantly reduced. To differentiate the two, we need to define some terms.

There are teachings on suffering in a lot of different traditions, both secular and religious. No discussion of pain and suffering, for me, can happen without at least a nod to Buddhism and its language of suffering.

When we say that the Buddha taught, "All life is suffering, and the way to escape suffering is to embrace impermanence," he wasn't saying, "Please pretend you see no suffering; please pretend you aren't in pain." He wasn't saying, "If you'd just let go of your attachments, nothing would hurt." He saw suffering. He saw pain. He wanted to find a way to stay present and respond. To respond without flinching. Without turning away from the abyss of pain present in the world.

The Buddha saw pain. He asked: "What can I do to not lose my mind and my heart, here? How can I keep both eyes and heart open without being consumed by this? How can I keep my gaze steady on that which cannot be fixed?"

His response—in my mind anyway—was love. Love with open hands, with an open heart, knowing that what is given to you will die. It will change. Love anyway. You will witness incredible pain in this life. Love anyway. Find a way to live here, beside that knowledge. Include that knowledge. Love through that. Be willing to not turn away from the pain of this world—pain in yourself or in others.

The practices and tools we have from Buddhism and other traditions are meant to help you withstand the pain of life, to keep your eyes on the broken place without being consumed by it. They aren't meant, as pop-psychology might have us believe, to remove all pain so that you can remain "happy."

They're meant to reduce suffering in the face of pain, not remove pain itself.

Suffering and pain are not the same thing. And that distinction is the beginning of true healing and support inside your grief.

■ ■ ■

As we've said, pain is a healthy, normal response when someone you love is torn from your life. It hurts, but that doesn't make pain *wrong*.

Suffering comes when we feel dismissed or unsupported in our pain, and when we thrash around inside our pain, questioning our choices, our "normalcy," our actions and reactions.

Suffering comes with being told to not feel what you feel. Suffering comes with being told there is something wrong with what you feel. Suffering comes with all the crap that gets loaded on us by friends and colleagues and random strangers who, with the best of intentions, correct, judge, or give advice on how we need to grieve better. Suffering also comes when we don't eat, don't get enough sleep, spend too much time with toxic people, or pretend we're not in as much pain as we're in. Suffering comes when we rehash the events that led up to this death or this loss, punishing ourselves for not preventing it, not knowing more, not doing more. Suffering brings with it anxiety, and fear, and isolation.

If we want to make this better for you, your *suffering* is where we need to look for change.

THE GREAT GRIEF EXPERIMENT

Once we've made the distinction between pain and suffering, we still need to answer the questions of what we *do* about any of this. The broad answer is simple: pain gets supported; suffering gets adjusted. There is no one way to do either of these things. Your grief is as individual as your love. Your way through this will be made by you, in ways that are unique to your mind, your heart, your life.

It helps if you think of it not as something you can do correctly or incorrectly, but instead as an ongoing experiment. No matter how many times pain or grief has entered your life, this time is the first time. This grief is unlike any other. Each new experience gets to unfold—and be tended—in the ways that best suit what hurts.

You'll need to find out what those best ways are, in order to withstand your loss. You'll need to identify what is pain and therefore needs support, and what is suffering and can therefore be changed. You'll need to ask yourself questions and experiment.

THIS IS NOT A TEST

You might hear that whatever has happened is a test, whether that's meant as a test of your faith, or your practice, or your emotional stability. I think that sets you up. A "test" implies that the universe is cruel, that you've been thrown into an impossibility and are being watched to see if you can figure it all out. Watched to see how much pain you're in and how you're handling it. Watched to see how well you address your own suffering. Watched to see if you can do this right.

This is not a test.

Your grief is not a test *of* love; it's an experiment *in* love. There's a huge difference between the two. Experimental faith, experimental relationship with yourself, with this life, with grief, with pain, with love, with suffering—it's all an experiment. It's not a test. You can't fail. You haven't failed.

The point of any practice, the point of this experiment, is to be the strongest, most whole vessel you can be to hold what is, to live this life that's asked of you. Whether we're talking about pain or about suffering, the underlying orientation is the same: allow yourself to experiment, to find what helps, to find what makes things just a little easier. Not because doing so will make this OK, but because doing so makes this gentler on you.

There is no one correct way to live this. Others have come before you, and others will come after, but no one carries grief—or love—in the same way you do. Grief is as individual as love. There's nothing to do *but* experiment.

It's all a work in progress.

GATHERING DATA

Experimenting in grief means looking for things that bring even the tiniest amount of relief or peace in your heart, or your life. We're talking micro-distinctions here: What gives you the strength or the courage or the ability to face the next minute, the next five? Does it feel better to write out your pain, or does that make you feel worse? Are you more inclined to sleep through the night if you go for a walk, or not?

Honestly, thinking about my own grief, choosing experiments in those early days was not a conscious thing. But thinking of grief *as* an experiment helped me. It let me know that there was no right way or wrong way, even for me, even inside myself.

One of the first things you can do inside your grief is to start paying attention to subtle shifts in how you feel. There are times that tears leak out at inopportune moments, times when the screaming inside you can't be held in, situations where holding yourself together is an entirely impossible task and rabid mind-loops keep replaying the events of your loss. These levee-breaking moments don't just happen—they build. The effects of both pain and suffering are cumulative.

While we might think that grief erupts without warning, there are always early warning signs. Gathering data helps you recognize those signs.

The first concrete practice, then, is to start a log of what you notice. At first, this will be an exercise in deconstruction after the fact. If you take a recent experience of feeling completely overwhelmed in your grief, can you look back over the week before it happened and see signs that the load was getting too heavy? Where were the additional stressors, the things that eroded your capacity to find rest or stability? What were some smaller eruptions that happened leading up to the larger one?

For me, an early warning sign was increased irritation with humans, animals, and inanimate objects. Simple things going wrong had a huge effect on me: as I got more overwhelmed, smaller and smaller things upset me. When I felt more stable, I had a much easier time brushing off swirling, annoying things.

Using this example, irritation was a sign that I needed to step back from arbitrary stressors in my life. It meant I probably needed more sleep, more food, and less contact with humans. The more I noticed these smaller indicators, the better I was at caring for myself. I could see them as cues that I needed to step back, make my world smaller and more care focused, rather than push myself.

If you think of your stability, your capacity to be present to this grief, as a bank account, every interaction is a withdrawal. Every stressor is a withdrawal. Recognizing the signs that your account is getting low is one big way of preventing—and soothing—both meltdowns and grief overwhelm.

Gathering data also helps you make micro-comparisons of better and worse: Are there times you feel more stable, more grounded, more able to breathe inside your loss? Does anything—a person, a place, an activity—add to your energy bank account? Are there activities or interactions that make this feel just a little softer or gentler? What's going on before and during those times? Conversely, are there activities or environments that absolutely make things worse? What elements contribute to making things suck even more than they already do?

Check in with yourself; note how you feel at different times of day, under what circumstances. Map your social interactions, how much sleep you've had, what you're eating (or not eating), and how you spend your time. You don't have to be obsessive about this; broad sweeps can be as useful as minute detail.

If you're unsure how to get started, you might ask yourself questions, like: How do I feel after I see this person? Do I feel supported and centered, or crazy and exhausted? Are there times of day I feel calmer and more grounded? Are there certain books, or movies, or places that take the sharp edge off my mind, if only for a little while?

Your log might look something like this: *Went to the grocery store. It was crowded. Saw so and so. Felt horrible, overwhelmed. Too many memories in that place. Felt exposed. Protective, defensive. Went to N's party, was able to stay in the kitchen and do things to help: felt OK. Felt good to be around people, but not with them. Talked with my mother-in-law—as long as we talked about logistics for the memorial, I felt supported. Talking about anything else just devolved into craziness (note: avoid talking about feelings with her!). Went to the beach this morning. Felt companioned by something, like the water could hold everything. Ate sugar cereal for breakfast. And lunch. Felt like shit.*

Be sure to note what things gave you even the tiniest bit more peace of being or calm. Especially in very early grief, nothing is going to feel amazing. The weight of immoveable pain is simply too much. However, there might be moments where you feel steadier, less anxious, or are able to be gentler with yourself. Remember that we're aiming to reduce suffering and find ways to tend to pain. If you find *anything* that feels less bad (in early grief) or, eventually, even a little bit good (whenever that happens), pay attention to that.

Gathering this data helps you figure out your own personal distinction between pain and suffering. Remember, suffering is arbitrary. Mapping those subtle distinctions of what helps and what doesn't is mapping your own suffering: It lets you know what can be changed or avoided. It lets you know where you *do* have some control in your grief. Whenever possible, choosing to avoid those "things that don't help" decreases your suffering, making you more available to tend to your own pain.

GATHER GENERAL DATA

For the next week, keep a log of how you feel throughout the day, under different circumstances, in various places, and in various social situations. What do you notice?

EVIDENCE: THE OUTCOME IS MORE IMPORTANT THAN THE ACTION

How do you know when you're doing well, versus really floundering or suffering in your grief?

Because our metric can no longer be the cessation of pain, figuring out your relative wellness inside grief can be tricky. How do you know when you're emotionally stable, given the fact that you cry all the time? How can you tell if the pain you feel is because of the actual loss, or because you're stuck in a loop of blaming yourself for everything?

The data gathering you did in the last exercise assists you in recognizing your early warning signs and lets you see more clearly what helps and what doesn't. But in intense grief, it can be hard to actually tell the difference between "doing well" and making things worse. It can be hard to separate pain from suffering.

In that case, it's helpful to look at the outcome of certain actions, identifying the signs of suffering, and the signs of comparative calm.

Even though every grief is unique, there are several broad indicators:

Evidence of suffering: poor sleep, no appetite, excessive appetite, nightmares, intrusive thoughts, anxiety, self-judgment, emotional reactivity (reactivity is different from grief or pain), short temper, sense of guilt disproportionate to actual responsibility, inability to breathe through intense emotion or to compartmentalize intensity enough to care for yourself, feeling victimized by your own pain or by the responses of others, a sense that your pain is too large to be contained or survived.

Evidence of relative calm: emotional evenness, self-kindness, sense of being held or companioned inside your pain, validation, feeling somewhat rested, eating enough for your body's needs, feeling an acceptance of your emotional state (no matter what that state is), ability to respond to others' poor behavior with clear redirection or correction, taking things less personally, ability to compartmentalize intense emotion or remove yourself from a situation in order to tend to that emotion, sense of connection to self, others, and those you've lost.

NOTING THE EVIDENCE

As part of your experiment in grief, it can be helpful to make a list like this for yourself: On one side of the page, make a list of signs you're really suffering. On the other side, a list of signs that you're caring for yourself well. What is evidence of suffering for you (for example, not sleeping well, feeling extra irritable, etc.)? What evidence shows that you're doing the best you can to tend to your pain (for example, feeling rested, able to more easily ignore or shrug off small annoyances, etc.)?

WELLNESS VERSUS WORSENESS

One of the biggest causes of suffering in grief is the self-harm we do to ourselves with our thoughts.

(Did you just say, "OMG, yes!"?)

We'll talk more about specific mind-related challenges like anxiety, memory problems, and intrusive thoughts in other chapters, but now is a good time to bring up self-judgment, scrutiny, and blame.

In times of stress, your mind can get really ravenous and start eating itself. I know mine does. Insightful, self-reflective people tend to be far harder on themselves than other folks. In this instance, a sharp mind is not necessarily your friend. Especially in out-of-order or unusual death (but in many other losses as well), we rehash the events, and our roles in them, over and over and over. We process everything: every nuance, every word, every choice. I wrestled not only with what happened that day at the river, but also with the intractable mind-loops I got into nearly every day around how well or not well I was doing, whether or not Matt would think I was doing this well or not, and how unfair it was that I felt I was being judged by his invisible ghost in my mind, given what I had just gone through.

The mind. Not so much a happy place.

It's true what they say in many spiritual traditions: the mind is the root of suffering.

Even if some of what your mind tells you is true (and 99.9 percent of it is not one bit true), there is no reason to increase your suffering with an unrelenting series of cruel and judgmental thoughts. Imaginary unwinnable battles are not a kindness.

■ ■ ■

So how do you sort the not-useful thoughts from the useful thoughts? The language is a little clunky, but I think of this as a practice of discerning wellness thoughts versus worseness thoughts. "Worseness" thoughts take your pain and grind more stress into it, increasing your suffering. You're going to have your own particular way of mentally tormenting yourself, but it's really just a manufactured anxiety about what might happen in the future or stressing about what happened in the past. What did I miss? Why didn't I do something differently? How am I supposed to live with this now? Did I cause all this? Those are the kinds of thoughts that shut you down and shut you off. They're not useful. They create suffering. They make things worse.

"Wellness" thoughts have the opposite effect: your pain still exists, but your sense of calm or stillness is increased. Wellness thoughts are the stories, ideas, and inner images that bring you closer to yourself. They bring you just the tiniest sense of peace or rootedness, increasing your capacity to withstand the pain you're in.

WELLNESS VERSUS WORSENESS

Drawing from some of what you identified in the last two exercises, create a side-by-side list of what makes you feel saner and what makes you feel crazy. What are the thoughts, ideas, or images that are on the worseness side of the equation? You can also add the activities from your earlier lists—things like spending time with certain people, spending too much time online, eating poorly. Basically, anything that pulls you away from love, pulls you away from kindness to yourself, or makes you feel completely nuts.

On the other side of the page, list wellness thoughts, ideas, images, and the activities that help you feel more rooted and calm. I'm not going to make any big guesses about what your list would look like. You know it when you feel these things. You know when you're in your own core. You know when things feel right in you.

Write these things out during a time of relative calm or quiet—that way, when your pain gets too large, you'll have something solid to refer to for help. Rather than court more suffering, you can redirect your thoughts toward wellness and gentleness or choose different actions from your list of things that don't make this worse.

What things increase suffering? Which allow you to hold your pain more gently?

WHAT DIFFERENCE DOES IT MAKE?

The reason I have you spend time gathering data is so that you can identify the times your suffering increases and the times your suffering is more quiet or manageable. Differentiating pain from suffering helps you understand the connection between certain activities and their impact on your grief. Recognizing which thoughts make this easier and which thoughts make this worse lets you more easily redirect your mind away from arbitrary suffering.

We can take the previous exercises—mapping your activities and interactions, evidence of suffering and tending this well, and wellness versus worseness—and create a compass of sorts, your guide to survival. Life coach Martha Beck calls this finding your own North Star. It's a way to both recognize your own evidence of suffering and give yourself a road map for how to decrease said suffering, especially when you're so lost in pain that you don't know what to do to help yourself.

As a composite document, it's a way to recognize when your pain is getting too heavy, too hard to bear: evidence of suffering is clear. It gives you a starting point of ideas for how to help yourself when your suffering is too much: choose activities that have helped induce a state of relative calm in the recent past. Not sleeping well? Your data may show you that reducing your sugar intake and staying off the computer late at night help you sleep a little better. Feeling consumed by rage and a sense of injustice? Your data might show that your justifiable anger gets much larger when you've spent time with "friends" who judge or dismiss your grief. To soothe that torment, you might spend time in the natural, nonhuman world, where you don't feel judged. You can choose to spend more time doing things that have even the slightest chance of inducing more calm or peace in you, and see how that goes.

THIS IS STUPID

All this talk of gathering data and creating a compass can start to seem like a ridiculous, cerebral exercise. And in some ways, that's exactly what it is. But here's the thing: you aren't meant to, nor are you made to, withstand pain like this with absolutely no tools and absolutely no way to help yourself. The only way to know what is likely to reduce your suffering is by becoming curious about it. Mapping the territory.

The best list in the world isn't going to actually fix anything. I know. Remember that this is an experiment. Creating a list of things that help and things that make this worse gives you a compass. It gives you a tangible point of orientation when the reality of life and loss gets too big for one person to contain. It won't fix anything. And it might help, if even just a little.

What we're trying for here, what I hope for you, is that you can find some peace in this for yourself, in this moment. That your suffering can be reduced. That you can tend to your pain, come to yourself with kindness. That you can hold your gaze on what is broken, without falling into the abyss of suffering that always makes things worse.

As you gather data and start to observe what makes things worse or even slightly less bad, you might see patterns begin to emerge. There are times you feel calmer and times you feel whipped around like a tetherball. One is not more right or more "emotionally evolved" than the other. One just feels better, and the other feels like crap. Sometimes you choose the crap because you don't have it in you to care for yourself. Totally valid. Do what you can.

Sometimes, with the small amount of energy you have, the only thing you can do is heave yourself in the direction of wellness. Heave yourself in the direction of gentleness-to-self. You don't have to do any more than that. Just turn toward it. Turn toward wellness—that's enough. It counts.

8

HOW (AND WHY)
TO STAY ALIVE

Using tools to reduce your suffering is one of the few concrete actions to take inside grief. Reducing suffering still leaves you with pain, however, and that pain can be immense.

Surviving early grief is a massive effort. Forget getting through the day; sometimes the pain is so excruciating, the most you can aim for is getting through the next few minutes. In this chapter, we review tools to help you bear the pain you're in, what to do when that pain is too much, and we explore why kindness to self is the most necessary—and most difficult—medicine.

GRIEF AND SUICIDALITY:
WHAT YOU NEED TO KNOW

Grief takes a toll on your mind, your body, your relationships—everything. The thought of endless months and years without the one you love is overwhelming. The thought of everyone else going back to their lives while you're still sitting there in the wreckage is overwhelming. The reality is just too big to let in. For many people, continuing to wake up each morning is a disappointment: *Damn, I'm still alive.* Thoughts like that make perfect sense.

Feeling like you'd rather not wake up in the morning is normal in grief, and it doesn't mean you're suicidal. Not wanting to be alive is not the same thing as wanting to be dead. It's hard to tell non-grieving people that, though, as people understandably get worried about your safety. And because people tend to get upset when we talk about not wanting to be alive, we just stop talking about it altogether. That's dangerous.

There's a reality here, inside intense grief, that we need to talk about directly. Sometimes you do not care one bit whether you live or die. Not because you're actively suicidal, but because you simply *do not care.* There are moments inside grief when it seems easier to just be reckless, let death happen, a sort of daring the universe to pick you off. Sometimes you do not care one bit about your own "safety." I know. All those encouragements from others about having so much to live for, that there's still goodness to come in your life—they feel irrelevant. They kind of are irrelevant. You can't cheerlead yourself out of the depths of grief.

Survival in early grief is not about looking toward the future. It's not about finding something that lights you up, or gives you a reason for living. It just doesn't work like that. Because those ordinary encouragements about the value of life are irrelevant, you'll need other ways to navigate those extra-intense times when grief threatens to overtake you.

My most intense moments of rather-be-dead feelings usually came while I was driving on the highway. What kept my hands on the wheel in those cannot-care-about-myself moments was knowing I did not want to create another me. I kept driving, or stopped driving, because I did not want to risk harming someone else. I would not chance creating another widow. I did not want to mess up someone else's life, or cause anyone else any pain, by creating an accident scene they had to clean up. Not wanting to create more pain for someone else was a strong enough motivation to make safer choices.

I also had a pact with a fellow widow: When we had those moments of overwhelming pain, we drew on the promise we made to each other to stay alive. To not be reckless. Not because the future was going to be so much better eventually, but because we didn't want to cause each other more pain. We needed each other. We needed to know that the other relied on us. Our love and commitment to each other got us through some truly terrible times.

There's a range inside grief from simply not wanting to be here to being seriously tempted to stop being here.

Feeling less than psyched about being alive is normal. It's important to have at least one person in your life to whom you can be honest about your disinterest in survival. Telling the truth can take some of that pressure off. And no matter how intense it gets, practice safety first. Please stay alive. Do it for yourself, if you can. Do it for others if you must.

Please note: Feeling like you'd rather not wake up in the morning is very different from thinking about actually harming or killing yourself. If you're thinking about harming yourself, please reach out for help. There are people who have been where you are. Survival can be one minute at a time. If you need help to make it through, please contact the suicide prevention help line in your local area. Most countries have national support lines, and help is always available anywhere there is Internet access.

> I'm not going to kill myself, but I can tell you that if a piano were falling from the roof of this building I'm walking past, I wouldn't rush to get out of the way.
>
> **DAN, after the death of his husband, Michael**

SURVIVING PAIN: KEEPING YOUR
EYE ON THE BROKEN PLACE

For physical issues, we have an entire pharmacopoeia of pain medicine. For the actual pain of grief, we have . . . nothing. It's always seemed so bizarre to me that we have an answer for almost every physical pain, but for this—some of the most intense pain we can experience—there is no medicine. You're just supposed to feel it.

And in a way, that's true. The answer to pain *is* simply to feel it. Some traditions speak of practicing compassion in the face of pain, rather than trying to fix it. As I understand the Buddhist teaching, the fourth form of compassion in the Brahma Viharas, or the four immeasurables, describes an approach to the kinds of pain that cannot be fixed: *upekkha*, or equanimity. Upekkha is the practice of staying emotionally open and bearing witness to the pain while dwelling in equanimity around one's limited ability to effect change. This form of compassion—for self, for others—is about remaining calm enough to feel everything, to remain calm *while* feeling everything, knowing that it can't be changed.

Equanimity (upekkha) is said to be the hardest form of compassion to teach, and the hardest to practice. It's not, as is commonly understood, equanimity in the way of being unaffected by what's happened, but more a quality of clear, calm attention in the face of immoveable truth. When something cannot be changed, the "enlightened" response is to *pay attention*. To feel it. To turn toward it and say, "I see you."

That's the big secret of grief: the answer to the pain is in the pain. Or, as e. e. cummings wrote, healing of the wound is to be sought in the blood of the wound itself. It seems too intangible to be of use, but by allowing your pain to exist, you change it somehow. There's power in witnessing your own pain. The challenge is to stay present in your heart, to your heart, to your own deep self, even, and especially, when that self is broken. Pain wants to be heard. It *deserves* to be heard. Denying or minimizing the reality of pain makes it worse. Telling the truth about the immensity of your pain—which is another way of paying attention—makes things different, if not better.

It's important to find those places where your grief gets to be as bad as it is, where it gets to suck as much as it does. Let your pain stretch out. Take up all the space it needs. When so many others tell you that your grief has to be cleaned up or contained, hearing that there is enough room for your pain to spread out, to unfurl—it's healing. It's a relief. The more you open to your pain, the more you can just be with it, the more you can give yourself the tenderness and care you need to survive this.

Your pain needs space. Room to unfold.

I think this is why we seek out natural landscapes that are larger than us. Not just in grief, but often in grief. The expanding horizon line, the sense of limitless space, a landscape wide and deep and vast enough to hold what is—we need those places. Sometimes grief like yours cannot be held by the universe itself. True. Sometimes grief needs more than an endless galaxy. Maybe your pain could wrap around the axle of the universe several times. Only the stars are large enough to take it on. With enough room to breathe, to expand, to be itself, pain softens. No longer confined and cramped, it can stop thrashing at the bars of its cage, can stop defending itself against its right to exist.

There isn't anything you need to do with your pain. Nothing you need to do *about* your pain. It simply is. Give it your attention, your care. Find ways to let it stretch out, let it exist. Tend to yourself inside it. That's so different from trying to get yourself out of it.

The way to come to pain is with open eyes, and an open heart, committed to bearing witness to your own broken place. It won't fix anything. And it changes everything.

TENDING TO PAIN: WHAT WOULD IT TAKE?

Most people don't intentionally ignore their pain. It's not that we don't want to bear witness to it; we're just not sure what it takes to face it. Just because giving grief space is a nonlinear, and therefore somewhat amorphous, skill doesn't mean it doesn't *take* skill.

My friend and colleague Mirabai Starr, author of *Caravan of No Despair*, writes in a blog post on her website:

> As we breathed into the truth of what had happened in our lives, safe in the protective community we built together, we began to discover that the unbearable became bearable, that by whispering "yes" instead of screaming "no," an ineffable grace began to fill the space of our shattered hearts. . . .
>
> Try it. If you've tried it before, try it again. Find the smoldering ache of loss inside of you and soften into it. Allow yourself to gently and lovingly explore exactly what it feels like to hurt in this way. With compassion for yourself, disarm your wounded heart and breathe quietly inside the wreckage. No need for fancy formulas or prescribed affirmations. No goal. Just be. Right here. Inside the fire of grief. One breath in front of the other.[1]

Mirabai encourages us to seek out the "smoldering ache of loss," but facing that pain head-on, coming to it gently, truly feeling the intensity of weight and shape can feel daunting. Even the idea of softening into the pain can be scary. What will you find there? If you soften into it, will you ever find your way back out?

Part of this process is learning to trust yourself. Trust is really tricky when the universe has upended itself, so I'm not talking about trust that everything will work out, or trust that you'll do everything right. Not at all. I'm talking more about trusting that you won't abandon yourself in your pain.

Sometimes, you just need to know that you *can* care for yourself. That, no matter what happens, you will show up for yourself as though you're someone you love, caring for yourself as best you can. Doing that repeatedly helps you strengthen your trust in yourself, and that, in turn, makes it easier to face your pain directly. It lets you seek out your pain, with the intention of seeing it with compassion.

In trauma work, we never dive into discussion of the actual traumatic events until the person has a solid framework of support and a way to manage the feelings that come up. Part of building your trust in yourself lies in creating that framework, adding safety to the prospect of looking for pain.

In order to go looking for your pain, to feel it directly and with love, what would it take? What would need to happen for you to feel safe or strong enough to soften into your pain? Time? Privacy? Wine? An anchor on the other side? A guarantee of outcome?

> If you want me to breathe in this wreckage, I have to lean into it, head-on. Place my whole weight in the wreckage, allow it to hold me up, hold me down. It means reliving every single moment. The hardest, darkest, sharpest ones. The happy ones before he died that bring a specific kind of pain. It means being pregnant all over again. Counting down the days. Filled with that exquisite excitement that is absolutely unique to the moment you meet your child.
>
> Sometimes I want to go looking for the pain. I want to marinate in it, allow it to soak into my skin. It's a tonic of sorts. A flush of the system. A way to demolish the foundation and start from nothing. Which sometimes—dare I say it—can make you

feel good on the other end. It rewards you to taste fearlessness. To have nothing to lose. The grief is disarming, but sometimes the afterward is intoxicating. Because what can you do to me now? This cockiness was hard-won. I'm new land craving to be built upon.

KATE SUDDES, Writing Your Grief student, on the death of her son, Paul

SUPPORT IN THE WRECKAGE

Finding out what you need in order to feel, not "OK" with all this, but somehow companioned and supported inside the wreckage, is the heavy work of surviving grief. To explore your own needs, you might write your responses to the questions below. Or you might respond to something else in Mirabai's passage. Whatever calls you, write into that.

- What would you need in order to feel more supported inside your pain? How can we make an impossible situation more kind, gentler, and easier on your heart?

- You might address your pain as a separate being: "In order to feel safe enough to face you, I would need . . ."

- You might begin a free write with the line: "If you want me to breathe in this wreckage . . ."

This is also a great exercise when you have an upcoming anniversary, or a difficult event on the horizon. Often, we can get through difficult things if we know there's an end point. You can make that end point for yourself by setting an activity or a date with a trusted friend for directly after whatever it is you need to get through. For example, if you know it's going to be extremely intense and emotional to meet with the estate lawyers, plan to meet a friend for tea, or a walk, after the meeting is done. Pack yourself some nourishing food for after the meeting. Queue up a ridiculous movie.

Answering the questions in the above writing prompt can give you a sense of what you need in order to feel well supported inside whatever crappy thing you have to face. Setting this up in advance gives you an anchor during the event and makes sure you have a net of support after the event. Taking care of yourself like this is like time travel—give your future self the support she needs now, so she doesn't have to ask for it later.

IT'S TOO MUCH!

The core "work" of grief really is learning to companion yourself inside it. But another equally important skill is in shutting off your grief, or your emotions, when it isn't safe to feel them. That might be because you're at work, or you're dealing with your kids/in-laws/parents/chatty neighbors, or you're trying to drive or operate machinery. Sometimes keeping your attention on the broken place is just too much to bear. I'm not talking about shutting down your emotions as a long-term solution (that *so* does not work), but shutting down in a moment where to feel the full intensity of your pain would not be beneficial. Denial is actually a kindness, at times. Distraction is a healthy coping strategy.

I remember the first Valentine's Day after Matt died. At this time, I was still so rarely eating, it was important to keep a lot of different quick-to-eat foods in the house, in case the urge to eat came up. I worked myself up to get to the grocery store. I noticed that the parking lot seemed especially crowded, but I pushed myself to go in. I was so completely detached from any events going on in the outside world, I had no idea it even *was* Valentine's Day. Once inside, I was instantly hit with couples couples couples everywhere. Couples in love, or seemingly in love, shopping together, arm in arm. Big signs proclaimed the romance of the day. Everywhere I turned, couples were lovingly discussing which wine to buy, or whether to spring for that expensive, organic, grass-fed steak.

Everywhere I turned, Matt was dead. Matt was dead. There are no more romantic dinners. There are no more mundane dinners. There is no more anything. And not only that, but each one of these loving partnerships will eventually end in death. The walls began to close in around me. I couldn't breathe. I couldn't hold back my tears.

I ran from the store, found my car, and somehow got inside before the floodgates broke. I knew I was in trouble. I was frantic. I needed the pain to stop. I knew I was not safe to drive. None of my normal support team picked up their phones or answered my texts. Of course not—they were with their partners or families on Valentine's Day.

Fortunately, my mind came up with an exercise I'd taught a million times in my practice before death entered my life: When your inner world is melting, focus on the tangible, external, physical world. Stop the meltdown. Calm your brain. Stop the spiral from continuing.

Instantly, old habits snapped into place. Find all the things that are orange, anywhere around you. Name them: Shoes. The printing on the odometer. The logo on that sign over there. That woman's jacket. Skateboard. Stupid, ugly bike. The background image on a stamp, poking out from a pile of mail on the passenger's seat.

I might have also chosen a letter of the alphabet and named all the things I could think of that started with that letter. Or counted the stripes in the parking lot. Or picked up the paper menu for the Thai restaurant that was on the floor of the car, naming the ingredients in my used-to-be favorite dishes. The objects themselves didn't matter. What did matter was that the objects I chose meant nothing to me, and looking for them, counting them, gave me an anchor inside an emotional storm I wouldn't be able to control if I turned to fully face it.

When your pain is too big for the environment you're in, it can turn into emotional flooding. Emotional flooding is not what we're going for when I suggest you make space for your pain. Pain is never going to feel good, but there are certainly times when the enormity of your reality is easier to tend to than others.

DON'T FOCUS ON YOUR BODY; DON'T TRY TO FIND YOUR "HAPPY PLACE"

When you need an anchor inside an emotional storm, it doesn't matter what physical thing you choose; it just matters that it be as benign and repetitive as possible. Sometimes, in situations like this, clinicians and teachers recommend focusing on your breath, or on sensations in your physical body. When you're dealing with death, injury, or chronic illness, however, turning attention to the physical body can make things much worse.

For the first year or two after Matt died, I couldn't follow meditations or visualizations that had me focus on my breath. When I tried, or was directed to do so, all I could see or feel or remember was that Matt's body had no breath. Putting attention into my body itself reminded me, viscerally, painfully, that Matt no longer had a body. That my own body could fail at any time.

Some teachings also suggest that you imagine yourself in your "happy place" when you're overcome with emotion. In early grief, a "happy place" is pretty well impossible to find. There is no place your loss does not touch. There is nothing that is not tied back to it. In my life before Matt died, my internal happy place was a spot by the river. My inner river was destroyed by the literal one; I could never go back and be soothed. For one client, any chance of imagining a happy place was obliterated by the fact that, now paralyzed, he could never actually be alone in a happy place, let alone get himself there.

When your life has been entirely imploded and rearranged, there is not one thing, not one happy, calming place, activity, or image that is not tainted, somehow.

I don't mean this as a downer but simply as a reality check: tools that work outside grief aren't always useful inside grief. That's why I have you focus on something mundane and ordinary: there is less chance of an exercise like this setting off more pain when you focus on what is boring, repetitive, and outside your body.

Remember that turning away from your pain when your pain is too big for the situation is a kindness. It's a way to pay attention, to tend to yourself with love and respect. Get yourself through the flood as best you can, and come back to your pain when you have the resources and capacity to do so.

KINDNESS TO SELF

I've mentioned kindness several times in this chapter.

Have you noticed?

If we boiled down everything in this book about how to survive intense grief, it would come down to this: show yourself kindness.

Caring for yourself, showing up with love and tenderness for your own excruciating pain—it won't fix anything that can't be fixed.

But for all you've lived, for all you've had to do—the phone calls, the decisions, the funeral plans, the life evaporated in an instant, all of everything you've had to live—you deserve kindness. You deserve the utmost care and respect. You deserve love and attention.

Try as they might, the people around you don't always show you that kind of love. The world itself, with its random acts of pain and violence and general stress, won't always show you that kind of love. But you can.

Let me be to my sad self hereafter kind.

PETER POUNCEY, *Rules for Old Men Waiting: A Novel*

YOU CAN BE KIND TO YOURSELF

Kindness is self-care. Kindness is recognizing when you need to back off a bit. It's allowing your pain to exist without judgment, in trusting yourself, and in saying yes to what helps and no to what does not. Kindness means not letting your own mind beat you up.

Self-kindness is seriously difficult. We can talk all day about how other people deserve kindness, but when it comes to ourselves? Forget it. We know too much about our own shortcomings, the ways we've messed things up, just how badly we're doing everything. We treat ourselves far more harshly than we would ever allow anyone else to treat us. Everyone struggles with this; it's not just you. For many people, being kind to others is far, far easier.

What if we loop back to the fourth form of compassion, upekkha, equanimity, that "calm quiet attention to what cannot be changed"? That describes kindness.

Grief requires kindness. Self-kindness. For all you have had to live.

Kindness-for-self might be allowing yourself to sleep as much as you need to, without yelling at yourself for it. It might be saying no to a social engagement. It might be turning the car around right after you've arrived in the parking lot, having decided that getting groceries is just too much for you to bear right now.

It might mean cutting yourself some slack, backing off of the demands you place on yourself. It might mean pushing yourself sometimes, taking yourself out of the softer nest of distraction into the bigger landscape of pain.

What kindness looks like will change, but your commitment to it? That's where your safety is. That's where stability exists, inside this wholly bizarre and shaken world. Knowing you won't leave yourself.

Kindness won't change anything, but it will make things easier on your mind and your heart. So today, if even just for a little while, can you offer yourself kindness? Can you take a moment to ask what being kind to yourself might mean?

Turn toward it, even if you can't make it all the way there. Turn yourself in the direction of kindness. Hold on to it.

TRY THIS You might write your response to this question: What would kindness to yourself look like today? This moment?

THE MANIFESTO OF SELF-CARE

Because kindness to self is so hard to practice, it's important to have daily, tangible reminders.

In therapy, we often remind people of the airplane safety analogy: in times of trouble or danger, put your own oxygen mask on first before you try to help others. Inside your grief, you *have* to put yourself first. To survive, you have to become fierce about caring for yourself.

A manifesto of self-care is a road map for survival. It's shorthand and course correction when you feel overwhelmed and lost in your grief. It's support and encouragement to stay true to yourself, to follow your own needs, when the outside world insists that you do things their way. It helps you choose kindness over self-flagellation.

Calling it a "manifesto" maybe seems inflated and self-important. But seriously—being fierce about your own needs, putting yourself first, insisting on making space for what makes this better, easier, gentler—nothing else is more important.

A manifesto of self-care can be as short as two words: practice kindness. It can also be a love letter to yourself or a list of ten or so things that are important to remember.

SELF-CARE MANIFESTO

If you created your own manifesto of self-care, what would it include? Write it out. Post it somewhere. Post it everywhere. Practice daily. No matter how many times you've slipped into suffering, or allowed your mind to beat you up, you can always return to kindness.

May you, to your own sad self, be kind.

9

WHAT HAPPENED TO MY MIND?

Dealing with Grief's Physical Side Effects

Descriptions of the many ways grief impacts your body and mind are not always easy to find. This chapter covers some of the most common—and strange—effects of grief and offers tools to help support and nourish your body and mind as you navigate the new landscape of life after loss.

GRIEF AND BIOLOGY

We often think of grief as primarily emotional, but grief is a full-body, full-mind experience. You're not just missing the one you've lost; your entire physiological system is reacting, too. Studies in neurobiology show that losing someone close to us changes our biochemistry: there are actual physical reasons for your insomnia, your exhaustion, and your racing heart.[1] Respiration, heart rate, and nervous system responses are all partially regulated by close contact with familiar people and animals; these brain functions are all deeply affected when you've lost someone close.

Grief affects appetite, digestion, blood pressure, heart rate, respiration, muscle fatigue, and sleep—basically everything. If it's in the body, grief affects it.

In addition to physical effects, cognitive changes, memory loss, confusion, and shortened attention spans are all common in early grief. Some effects even last for years—and that's perfectly normal.

It's true on so many levels: losing someone changes you.

BEING "IN-BETWEEN"

Early grief is a liminal time. Liminality (from the Latin word *līmen*, meaning "a threshold") is the quality of ambiguity or disorientation that occurs when a person is no longer who they once were and has not yet become someone entirely new and solid. This is one place where that commonly used transformation metaphor of a butterfly *is* helpful: we could say that while it's inside the cocoon, a caterpillar-butterfly is in a liminal state, neither caterpillar nor butterfly. In the same way, we are neither one thing nor another in early grief. Everything we've been—both physically and emotionally—is in a state of flux.

Your body and your mind are in an in-between state. Understanding what's going on can help you make choices that support your physical self as it reels from this loss.

EXHAUSTION AND INSOMNIA

Sleep—getting too much or too little—is a big thing inside grief. This chapter on grief and the body starts with sleep issues because not getting enough sleep, or getting consistently poor-quality sleep, affects the way your body and your mind process your loss. Sleep is a time of restoration for the body, and it's always the first place to look for improvement or comfort when things are completely falling apart.

In my early days, grief was on its own sleep schedule. I was often wide-awake at ten at night, or heading back to bed at ten in the morning, after only being up for an hour or so. When Daylight Savings Time ended that year, I didn't bother adjusting my clocks. The only thing they showed me during that first year (or more) of grief was that I seemed to wake up at the same time every night: 3:00 a.m.

I can't even count the sheer number of times I woke myself up by the sound of my own crying.

Getting "good enough" sleep is important, but grief rearranges your sleep: either keeping you up or reducing your "awake" hours to a short little window between long naps. When you do sleep, grief pokes its way through no matter how exhausted you are. Some people find that they wake up repeatedly at the time their loved one died. Others are woken up reaching into the empty space, jolted awake by finding it, indeed, empty. Many people have a hopeful, hazy moment on waking, thinking maybe this was all a dream, only to have reality crash in on them as their eyes fully open.

If you're wrestling with sleep issues, you're not alone. Sleeping all the time and never being able to sleep enough are both entirely normal inside grief.

If you find you need almost constant sleep—as much as other life demands allow—it's OK. Sleep as much as you can, when you can. It helps your body restore itself, keeping your physical body as strong, well, and healthy as it can be. It's not avoidance, or denial: it's restoration and respite.

If you can't sleep or you're shaken by a dream, don't fight it. Your body and mind are processing so much emotion. It's hard to fall into sleep in that kind of pain. As much as you are able, rest when you can, even if you can't fully sleep. There are certainly things you can do to encourage falling asleep, but as we all know, grief doesn't always follow predictable rules.

This is one area where your medical teams—both allopathic and integrative—can help. Talk with your trusted providers about ways to support more restful sleep.

DREAMS AND NIGHTMARES

Though sleep is even more necessary during intense grief than it is at other times, nightmares about your loss can make sleep something you'd rather avoid. Recurrent dreams, or dreams that have you delivering the news about death over and over, are actually a healthy and necessary part of grief.

They suck. I know.

And dream-state sleep is when our minds do the deep, heavy work of breaking down the reality of loss into absorbable pieces. Psychotherapist James Hillman writes, "Dreams tell us where we are, not what to do."[2] Nightmares don't bring solutions or offer portents for the future. They're the creative, associative mind trying to orient itself to this loss.

That doesn't make them any easier. Your entire system is working so hard to help you survive, and nightmares are often part of that process. It's healthy, and "healthy" just feels like shit sometimes.

I love what teacher Jon Bernie recommends here: Notice it; bring your awareness to it. But don't mess with it. Don't dive in and get sticky trying to analyze it. He's not talking about nightmares, but it applies. When you've had a grief nightmare, you might recognize it, name it, as your mind trying hard to process this loss. Something as simple as repeating to yourself, "My mind is trying to make space for this," can help calm your mind and soothe your nervous system when a grief nightmare wakes you.

PHYSICAL CHALLENGES: GRIEF AND THE BODY

Has the physical nature of grief surprised you?

I've heard from a lot of grieving people struggling with "mystery" pains and illnesses, all attributed to grief or stress. Heart palpitations, headaches, stomach pains, feeling faint or dizzy—while I am in no way a medical doctor, I can tell you these things appear to be quite common in grief, especially in the early days. (If you're concerned about physical symptoms, please do speak to your doctor. Just because they *can* be grief related doesn't mean they necessarily *are*.) After Matt died, I seemed to inherit his heartburn, his sciatica, his customary sore neck. None of these things were "mine" in my life before he died. Those adopted pains weren't the only changes to my physical body, either.

Going back into some of my journals from the early days of my own grief, I'm struck by how tired I was. How much physical pain I was in—sore muscles, headaches, phantom pains that could show up anywhere. I visited the emergency room no fewer than four times in the first two years—with violent stomach pains, chest pains, changing vision—and each time, tests revealed nothing.

Diagnosis: stress.

The effect of stress on the physical body is well documented. Out-of-order death, unexpected grief, massive life changes—it's the understatement of the century to say those things cause *stress*.

It makes sense that your physical body rebels: it can only hold so much.

Many people have noticed that it's their body—their physical reactions and sensations—that alert them to an emotionally heavy date on the calendar. You might not consciously know today is the seventeenth of the month, but you've been more exhausted and rather sick to your stomach all day. It's only when you look at the calendar that you recognize it: the seventeenth is when he entered hospice, or when you got the first phone call that she was missing.

The body remembers. The body knows.

In many ways, I think of the body as the vessel that holds this entire experience for you. That it cracks and breaks and otherwise shows signs of stress makes sense when we think of what it has been asked to endure.

WEIGHT CHANGES

"Wow! You look great! You've lost so much weight. Did you start running or something?"

"My partner died."

"Well, whatever you've been doing, keep it up! You look amazing."

There's no "normal" appetite in grief. Some people eat under stress; some people, like me, lose all interest in food. I dropped more than twenty pounds within the first few months. I simply did not eat. My nutrients came largely from the cream in my tea and the occasional cupcake. Every few days, I might eat a few bites of something more.

I was fortunate—there was no lasting damage to my physical body. I was also under my doctor's care at this time, and she let me know she would intervene if she felt I was in danger. Your body may respond differently. Some people develop serious, lasting physical challenges due to what we call "the grief diet." Complications from over- or undereating can include diabetes, elevated cholesterol, respiratory problems—all manner of things you've probably heard a million times. When you stop eating because food is nauseating, or eat constantly because you need *something* to do, your body has to work harder to stay level and grounded.

That said, I know there's not always a lot you can do about it. Encouragement to eat well always works better than shaming or force. Your body needs fuel to survive this. You might find that small doses of healthy, nutrient-dense food are more easily tolerated by your mind and body than full-on meals. You might give yourself alternative options (a nap, a walk, calling someone), rather than continue eating past the point of being hungry. Do what you can.

SELF-CARE

Physical self-care often takes a backseat during grief. It's hard to care one bit for a healthy diet, or be motivated to practice meditation or any other stress-reduction techniques. There can be a cavalier sense of "what's the use?" in taking care of your physical body, given what you know about sudden loss or random accident.

The thing is, tending the organism—the physical body—is one of the few tangible ways you really can change your experience of grief. Finding small ways to care for your physical body can reduce your suffering, even if it doesn't change your pain.

Remember that caring for your physical body is an act of kindness (and you deserve kindness). Do what you can, as you can. Refer back to your answers to the questions and exercises in chapter 7 to help you identify any patterns or habits that might improve your physical well-being: what's helped a few times might help again. And please be sure to check in with your health care providers if you have specific concerns about your body.

GRIEF AND YOUR BRAIN: WHY YOU AREN'T THE PERSON YOU USED TO BE

When Matt first died, I lost my mind—and not in the ways you might think.

I used to be a person who could read books. I used to have a really great memory. I used to be a person who could keep everything straight without notes or a calendar. I used to be a person who could do all these things, and suddenly I was putting my keys in the freezer and forgetting my dog's name and couldn't remember what day it was or if I had eaten breakfast. I couldn't read more than a few sentences at a time, and I usually had to go back and reread those same lines many times. Once a person both skilled in and excited by deep intellectual debate, I could no longer follow even the simplest of discussions. I didn't understand how to give a cashier the correct change.

My mind simply stopped functioning. Has that happened for you? Have you lost your mind?

In the widowed world, we often use the term *widowed brain* (though it occurs in many different losses)—it's a great term for the cumulative cognitive effects of grief. If grief has recently erupted in your life—and by recently, I mean anything from yesterday to a few years ago—you will most likely find that your brain just does not work. You may have been brilliant and organized before this loss, able to multitask, remember, execute.

But grief changes all of that.

FIRST THINGS FIRST: YOU AREN'T CRAZY

If your mind is not what it used to be, you're entirely normal.

You are not crazy. You *feel* crazy because you're inside a crazy experience. Grief, especially early grief, is not a normal time. It makes perfect sense that your mind doesn't work the way it used to: everything has changed. Of course you're disoriented. Your mind is trying to make sense of a world that can no longer *make* sense.

Because of the way grief impacts the mind and cognitive processes, you've probably also lost interest in things you used to enjoy, your intellectual faculties may have changed, and your memory and attention span may be virtually nonexistent.

Grief does that. It rearranges your mind. It takes away skill sets you've had since childhood. It makes even the simplest things hard to follow. It makes once-familiar things feel arbitrary or confusing. It impacts your memory, your ability to communicate, your capacity for interaction.

While all these are completely normal, it can make you feel like you've lost many of the internal, personal things that made you, you.

MEMORY LOSS

There's a clumsy forgetfulness, or absentmindedness, that often comes with grief. Misplaced—or weirdly placed—keys and glasses are seriously common. Frozen food gets put in the dishwasher upon return from the grocery store. You show up at the dentist on Monday when your appointment is next week, on Thursday.

No matter how your short-term memory worked before your loss, it has likely changed in your grief. Forgetting names, missing appointments, not being able to remember if you gave the dog his medicine this morning—all normal. It's as if remembering all those little details are "extra" expenses, and your mind can't afford them. Your mind can only retain so many things, so it simply drops what is not necessary for survival. It's like triage in the mind.

This is another of grief's physical side effects that does seem to consistently improve over time. As you live further from the event of your loss, your mind will make more space for memory. Order will more or less be restored (or re-created).

In the meantime, leaving yourself multiple reminders and notes is a good way to outsource your memory. Your need for multiple sticky notes, timers, and alarms is not a sign that you aren't doing well. It's proof that you're doing whatever you can to support your mind and make things easier for yourself. Cover the entire house in reminders if that's what you need to do. They won't help you find your keys, but they might help you remember other things.

MENTAL EXHAUSTION

You may have been a massively productive person in your life before loss. Now you can barely get one thing accomplished in the hours you're awake. You might feel overwhelmed at the sheer number of details needing your attention. Many people feel they've lost their competence, their drive, and their former confidence.

There's a reason you can't get as much done as you used to.

Think of it like this: Let's say you have one hundred units of brain power for each day. Right now, the enormity of grief, trauma, sadness, missing, loneliness, takes up ninety-nine of those energy units. That remaining one unit is what you have for the mundane and ordinary skills of life. That one remaining circuit is responsible for organizing carpools and funeral details. It's got to keep you breathing, keep your heart beating, and access your cognitive, social, and relational skills. Remembering that cooking utensils belong in the drawer, not the freezer, that your keys are under the bathroom sink where you left them when you ran out of toilet paper—these things are just not high on the brain's priority list.

Of course you're exhausted. Your mind, like the rest of you, is doing the best it can to function and survive under very severe circumstances. Please try not to judge your current accomplishments based on what you *used* to be able to do. You are not that person right now.

TIME LOSS

As you look back on your day, you may not be able to articulate what you've done or accomplished. When asked, you likely cannot give any evidence of having *done* anything. Remember that much of the work of early grief is done inside your heart and mind, not in outward actions. That you have no idea what day it is, or can't remember when you last ate, makes perfect sense. It's in those lost, seemingly unproductive sections of time that your body and mind are attempting to integrate your loss: it's almost like an awake sleep cycle. You mind goes offline so it can heal.

Again, we return to the idea of tending your physical organism: care for yourself as best you can, and know that the fog of daily time loss will eventually clear. Allowing the lost time, yielding to it, rather than fighting it, can make it all a little easier.

READING AND NOT READING

All my life, I've been a voracious reader. Books have always been my most constant form of support and kinship. But for at least the first year after Matt died, I could barely read a label, let alone sustain my attention for a whole book. When I did read, I found myself not understanding. Well, not exactly not "understanding." I recognized the words. I knew what I was reading. But nothing sank in. It often took several tries with one paragraph to know where I was. Characters confused me. Storylines didn't make sense. I would get to the end of a line, forgetting what the first part had said.

I hear the same thing from just about everyone in grief's early days: grief obliterates their ability to read, comprehend, and sustain attention. Forget reading several books at once, as you used to. Reading one chapter—even one page—is emotionally and mentally taxing.

In fact, in writing this book, my team and I argued about how long the chapters should be. Knowing how difficult it is to read and comprehend, we went back and forth over the length of each chapter. There's so much to say about grief, and only so much capacity to take it all in.

No matter how much of a book person you were before your loss, your capacity to read has most likely been impacted by grief. There's not much you can do about that. For some, their comprehension returns, but their attention span never returns to its pre-loss state. For many others, comprehension and attention span gradually return, but their areas of interest in reading and learning take a completely new path.

If you're grieving this secondary loss of your reading ability, know that, in most cases, it is transitory. It just takes longer than you might think to regain (or rebuild) your reader's mind.

ON CONFUSION

Comprehension in reading isn't the only thing impacted by grief. In those early months, the world itself can become a bizarre and confounding place: I remember standing in the checkout line at the grocery store completely confused by the money in my hand. I'd lost the ability to count. I couldn't understand which bills meant what. I made a guess, tears streaming down my face, and handed a wad of money to the cashier.

Mental confusion and a sort of brain-fog feeling are extremely common. It's as if all our arbitrary human constructs—things like money, time, rules for driving (and other things), social expectations, levels of hygiene—seem utterly unrelated to anything we're living.

For a time, we are unhinged from the cultural forms we've laid down in human life. Things we agree to as a culture—like pieces of paper being fair trade for groceries, or lunchtime being at noon—are revealed as empty symbols, unrelated to anything intrinsically . . . real.

Grief strips life down to its irreducible essentials. In that visceral state, your distance from the "normal" world can feel insurmountable. There's an uncomfortable truth here: you are not like other people. Not right now.

The world has been split open. Things "ordinary," non-grieving people do as a matter of course will not always make sense, or feel meaningful, to you.

Whether it lasts a moment, or feels interminable, your confusion is normal. It does tend to ebb and flow, in relation to other stressors in your life, emotionally heavy tasks you have to complete, and how well you're eating and sleeping. This is why we go back to tending your physical body as bedrock: supporting the body can help reduce the signs of grief's addling effect on your mind.

CREATING NEW COGNITIVE PATHWAYS

I'm not a brain scientist by any stretch, but the way I understand it, our minds work by creating relationships and recognizing patterns. New information comes in, and the brain connects it to what we already know. Normally this process is seamless: you never really notice it.

In grief, your brain has to codify and collate an impossible new reality into itself. The data presented doesn't make any logical sense. There has never been anything like this event, so there is no way to connect or relate it to anything else. It doesn't fit. The brain cannot *make* this new reality fit. Like your heart, your brain resists this loss—it can't possibly be true.

Those blips and gaps in your memory and thought process are the brain trying to make data fit into a world that cannot absorb that data. Eventually, it will understand that this loss can't fit inside the structures that used to be. It will have to make new pathways, new mental relationships, wiring this loss into the person you are becoming, every day.

You aren't crazy. You aren't broken. Your brain is busy, and it will simply take a while to come back online.

Eventually, your mind will realize that car keys do not belong in the freezer.

Eventually, you will read whole lines again, whole paragraphs, without having to repeat the words to yourself so you understand.

Grief itself won't make sense, loss itself will not rearrange into something orderly and sensible, but your mind, and your heart, will adapt. This loss will be absorbed and integrated.

It's what your heart and mind are made for: adapting to new experiences. Not good, not bad—it is simply what they *do*.

For a lot of people, it's a few years before their entire cognitive capacity comes back to any recognizable form. There are losses in that, too. Some of those losses are temporary and some of them mean your mind is just different as you move forward. The thing to remember is that your brain is working hard to make sense of something that can't ever make sense. All those mental circuits that used to fire so clearly are trying their best to relate to this entirely changed world.

Your mind is doing the best it can to keep a bead on reality when reality is crazy. Be patient with yourself. Remember that this is a normal response to a stressful situation; it's not a flaw in you.

You're not crazy. You're grieving. Those are very different things.

RECOGNIZE GRIEF'S PHYSICAL AND MENTAL SIDE EFFECTS

What physical symptoms have you noticed in your grief?

How has grief changed the way your mind works?

If you're outside that initial impact of grief, how have you noticed your mind changing, as you become more accustomed to the weight of grief?

Validation is powerful inside grief. What's it like to hear stories (here and elsewhere) that show you that your experience is normal?

10

GRIEF AND ANXIETY

Calming Your Mind
When Logic Doesn't Work

Grief changes your body and your mind in strange ways. Cognitive capacity isn't the only brain function that gets wonky. Anxiety—whether it's new to you, or you experienced it before your loss—is a huge issue in grief.

I used to struggle a lot with anxiety.

Driving home from grad school late at night, my tired brain would conjure all manner of horrible, horrible images: things I was helpless to stop from where I was, still hours away from home. I'd imagine I'd left the stove on twelve hours earlier, and the house had burned down. Maybe it was burning right now. Images of my animals suffering flashed in front of my eyes.

It was awful.

With a lot of self-work, insight, and just plain irritation with that pattern, I found ways to manage those fears. In fact, I became so good at redirecting those thoughts that I felt I'd completely moved on. I hadn't had a freak-out like that in well over a decade.

In the months before Matt drowned, I noticed those fears coming back. I would leave the house and begin to panic that the cats would escape, get stuck somewhere, and die cold and alone and afraid. Or that our dog would get hit by a car, and I wouldn't be there to help. I started to worry whenever Matt was late calling. I'd spin off into imaginary negative fantasies instead of focusing on whatever was actually going on.

I caught myself in a fearful thought-spiral one day in early July. Out loud, I said, "Stop!" Out loud, I said what I have told myself a thousand times and have told clients over and over again: "Worrying about what has not happened is not useful. If something bad does happen, you will deal with it then. It is highly unlikely that anything awful will happen. If it does, you will deal."

Seven days later, the highly unlikely did happen. And you know what? My fear sensors never made a sound. No panic. No anxiety that morning. Nothing. I'd felt entirely, perfectly calm. When I needed my acute sensitivity to all things dangerous and bad, it failed.

In the years following, my anxiety went through the roof. I imagined more bad things happening. I imagined everyone I loved disappearing in an instant, everyone I knew and loved (including myself) in danger, suffering, dead. I was alert for any small indication that things were about to go wrong. It didn't matter that anxiety had proven itself highly ineffective in predicting or preventing catastrophe. Anxiety is an addictive drug, made all the more powerful by knowing that unlikely shit *does* happen, and there is nothing you can do.

I tell you this story because I bet you can relate.

Feelings of anxiety are normal for those who have survived an intense loss or trauma. Inside your grief, the whole world can feel like an unsafe place, one that requires constant vigilance: searching for early warning signs of trouble, guarding against more loss. You rehearse what you would do if you were faced with unthinkable trauma *again*.

If you're struggling with anxiety inside your grief, maybe you've tried to calm yourself down by thinking positive thoughts, by reminding yourself of the goodness all around you, or by asserting the typical safety of everyday life. But those things no longer work when you've already lived the unlikely. Freak accidents, out-of-order deaths, horrible, nightmare events—these things happen. To us. To me. To you. Anxiety, grief, and prior experience are a tricky combination. You don't trust your instincts anymore. Terrible things are possible. Constant vigilance can seem like the only route to take. Danger lurks everywhere. Loss is always waiting for you. You have to be prepared.

The problem is, rather than helping you feel safe, perpetual fear creates a small, hard, painful life that isn't safer than any other life. Your mind becomes an exquisite torture chamber. The future rolls out in front of you in a stream of horrible things. You can't sleep because of your anxiety, and your anxiety gets worse because you aren't sleeping. It's an incessant hamster wheel of fears, attempts at logic, and memory of things gone wrong.

Anxiety is exhausting. It sucks. And it's not even useful, no matter how much it screams that it's real. Anxiety is patently ineffective at managing risk and predicting danger. Most of our fears never come to pass, and as I wrote above, in true emergencies, anxiety is often conspicuously absent.

If anxiety is such a poor predictor of reality, why do we do it? What is it about anxiety that makes is seem so real, so logical, and so impossible to turn off?

BRAINS DO WHAT THEY DO . . . TOO WELL

Here's the thing: our mind is *made* to imagine dangerous scenarios. It's actually quite brilliant: we're programmed to envision things in the safety of our mind that we could never risk with our physical bodies. We run scenarios to assess risk, to work out what we might do in a certain situation, to puzzle out how we'd solve a life-or-death problem, so that we don't have to try out those risks with our much more fragile physical selves. On a less life-threatening basis, our brains work out what we'd do with everyday problems as a way to reduce the stress load on the body itself: you think through a problem, finding ways to make things easier or more manageable.

The brain is an internal problem-solving survival mechanism. It's beautiful.

When there is clear and present danger, our brains unleash a cascade of hormones meant to help us quickly escape. The nervous system shifts into high alert. The healthy, well-functioning brain helps us either escape the danger or fight off whatever has threatened our safety. Once the danger has passed, the body is meant to return to its calm, non-anxious, low-stress state.

That cascade of hormones and the resulting flight-or-fight response can also be triggered when we *imagine* stressful, dangerous, or threatening situations. Sometimes imagining a realistic potential danger is useful. The problem, though, is that, especially when we've already experienced a truly dangerous situation, we overuse those great imaginative skills. Each time we imagine multiple *potential* disasters, horrible dangers, all the ways the world can go wrong, we tell our nervous system that there is a current clear and present danger. We cue that flood of hormones that would help us escape. You can't run from an imagined danger, so those stress hormones never dissipate. You imagine more and more and more danger, cueing the body to spring into action it will never take; you never get back to "calm and relaxed."

We push our brains into exhaustion, trying to keep ourselves safe.

It's like a dog chewing at a hotspot—gnawing at the rash makes it itch more, which makes him chew on it more, which makes it itch more. Fear thoughts create a brain response, which creates a body response, which conditions your thoughts to come up with more fears, which starts the cycle again.

And this is why you can't talk yourself out of anxiety. It's also why you will never run out of terrible problems to solve: your mind is caught in a loop of its own making, always coming up with new threats to manage.

IMAGINING DANGER IN ORDER TO FEEL SAFE

If it's both ineffective and horrendous to live with, why do we do this to ourselves? It doesn't make logical sense, does it? Honestly, what we're looking for—in any kind of anxiety—is proof of safety. Whether that means physical safety or emotional safety, we all want to know we're safe, cared for, and won't be left alone, unloved, or unprotected. Our mind runs scenarios, often repeatedly, of *not* being safe—of being hurt in some way—so that we can find some scenario, some evidence, that proves we're safe.

In a weird sort of way, it's an understandable response: something in your mind says, "I'm scared," and your brain responds with a cascade of images and hormones to help you find safety. Because you've experienced the world as drastically unsafe at one point, when one fear gets resolved, your mind comes up with another fear, in a perpetual bid for safety: it's a natural survival tool on tilt.

Of course you're anxious. After a death or other massive loss, the whole concept of "safety" gets really sketchy. You can't rely on old comforts of believing that your fears are unlikely to come true. You can't lean on the statistically low risk of certain illnesses or accidents happening. Just because you saw your people half an hour ago does not mean they're still OK *now*. When the ordinary safety of the world has already failed you, how can you ever feel safe here again?

It's not that anxiety is *wrong*; it's more that it's not effective in creating the safety you seek. Here's the thing: no matter what your anxiety tells you, rehearsing disaster will not make you safe. Repeatedly checking in with people to be sure they're *still* safe will never create a lasting sense of safety.

SHORT-TERM APPROACHES TO ANXIETY

Because anxiety is a survival mechanism run amok, it won't work to just tell yourself to stop it: if you deny your fears, they will get louder. You can't apply logic to a fear-based system. It also won't work to wrap up everyone you love in a protective bubble and never let them out of your sight. Rather than suppress your fears, or frantically try to make the world around you safe, there are other things you can do to enhance your inner sense of security while maintaining a state of alert calm.

Since you're reading this chapter, I assume you're dealing with active anxiety. During active anxiety, it's not always helpful to do some of the more complex practices later in this chapter. Those approaches will help you retrain your mind to a more stable, neutral pattern so that you don't get lost in anxiety as often. But what if you're already in it? Soothing your mind when you're already in an anxiety-spiral and practicing self-care can help in the short term.

Soothe the System

Remember that anxiety is a brain-based, nervous system response to imagined danger. It's not logical; it's *biological*. Studies in both trauma sciences and neurobiology show that modifying your breathing helps soothe your nervous system when it's agitated, as it is during acute anxiety. I could totally geek out on all the cutting-edge brain science here, but what's really important is very simple: lengthening your exhale soothes your nervous system, shutting down the flood of stress hormones that trigger anxiety.

When you feel anxious, make your exhale longer than your inhale.

It really is that simple. And that's a good thing—because when you are actively freaking out, remembering one simple direction is far easier than remembering a whole slew of other interventions. Making your exhale longer than your inhale soothes the flight-or-fight response in the nervous system, and the focus on your breath gives you an anchoring thought in your mind rather than chasing one fear thought to the next. That it's simple is great: one option, under your control, always accessible.

During acute anxiety ("acute" meaning your brain is a tangled mess of fear) you might also consider some of the anchoring and calming exercises we talked about in chapter 8. If you pair one of those with lengthening your exhale, you'll help both your body and your brain find a still, calm place.

Did you just panic at the thought of being calm because you might miss something dangerous?

Remember that calming your anxiety is not one bit related to whether something unexpected happens or not. Calming your anxiety is about only that: *calming your anxiety*. The crazy train of fear prevents you from being present to what is, and it most definitely keeps you from enjoying whatever goodness is here in this moment. Anxiety also depletes your energy reserves, makes sleep difficult, and, in general, feels like crap. I don't want that for you.

If you take nothing else from this chapter, practice making your exhale longer than your inhale. It doesn't even have to be a deep breath: just exhale for a moment longer. Experiment with it. See how it goes.

Tend the Organism

Recognizing anxiety as a *symptom* of something rather than a predictor of reality is a useful distinction. For many people, anxiety increases when they're overtired, not eating well, or exposed to multiple challenges. If you know that your anxiety is connected to how you're feeling physically and emotionally, you can look for early warning signs—parallel markers—that let you intervene before it gets crazy.

The easiest approach is to refer back to the lists you made in chapter 7: that's where you'll find your early warning signs. As your thoughts become more anxious or agitated, it's a cue that you need to turn in, slow down, and care for your physical organism: sleep, eat, rest, move. Addressing these physical needs first can actually reduce a lot of your anxiety.

LONGER-TERM RESPONSES TO OVERCOME ANXIETY

Figuring out what to do when anxiety wraps you up in knots is important. When you're inside an anxiety spike, it's much more useful to help yourself calm down than it is to investigate the reasons behind it. Transforming your overall response and reaction to life from one of anxiety to a more calm and even state takes some practice, but it's not impossible. There are things you can do to help your overall system not fall into those anxiety habits so easily. Reducing the frequency and overall amount of anxiety you experience has three parts: learning to trust yourself, replacing disaster scenarios with more positive images, and finding a neutral place—neither denying danger nor succumbing to rampant anxiety.

Presume a Skilled Response

Anxiety is a manufactured feeling state that has nothing to do with current reality: it thrives in an imagined (negative) future. If you keep coming up with imaginary problems, your mind will keep providing imaginary solutions. Because the solution to each scenario is different, the anxious mind will try to cover all possible "what-if" situations, attempting to defuse each one in turn. In a relentless search for safety, it feeds on itself.

Here's an example: one of my clients is an intelligent, resourceful, calm, and diligent person. After her husband died, she began to obsess about things going wrong in her house, about changing jobs, about whether or not to travel, and any number of other things. She would lie awake at night wondering if she had set the heating system properly. If she had, was it actually working correctly? What would happen if it failed? What if the smoke detectors failed, or the furnace randomly blew up?

One after the other, her mind came up with new disasters. If she solved one, another popped up in its place. That's the problem with anxiety: you never run out of potential disaster.

Rather than continue to run successive disaster scenarios, coming up with an action plan for each and every one, it's far more effective and efficient to . . . trust yourself. In the face of multiple challenges presented by your mind, you might say: "I trust myself to handle any problem that comes up with the house. If there's something I don't know how to solve, I trust myself to ask for help."

Self-trust is tricky, but no matter what, you've got a bank of success stories to draw from. Large or small, you've likely proven that you can face most kinds of challenges. There is no reason to believe you wouldn't be able to solve these problems yourself, or ask for help if needed.

There's also the fact that putting out imaginary fires does absolutely nothing to help you prepare for any actual fire. If you have anxiety over specific things, see if you can identify ways you can lessen the risk of those things happening. Do practical, realistic things, like changing the batteries in your smoke alarms, locking your doors at night, and wearing your bike helmet. Address your fears in concrete ways, but don't let your fears keep you captive. Until and unless an actual need arises, there is no reason to run disaster scenarios.

Instead of creating trouble out of nothing, you might tell yourself: Right now, as far as I know, everything is fine. If a challenge arises—of any kind—I trust myself to respond with skill. If there's something I don't know how to do, I trust that I'll ask for help.

Using a blanket statement of self-trust increases your sense of security far more effectively than running potential disaster-solution patterns. Over time, you can retrain your mind to self-soothe rather than self-implode.

■ ■ ■

"But," you might say, "I seriously *failed*!" Self-trust can feel impossible when loss has shown up in your life. In cases of accident, suicide, prenatal loss, and other losses, it's normal to question yourself. What doesn't help, though, is persecuting yourself from now through all eternity. Maybe you could have done something different. Maybe. And maybe you did what you could with the information you had at the time. And maybe this loss truly had nothing to do with what you "missed," and you couldn't have changed the outcome.

Regardless of what's accurate, it does you no good to move through the rest of this life afraid to miss something. Courting that kind of perpetual anxiety will only exhaust you to the point where you can't respond with any skill or insight when you actually do need it.

A calm mind and a well-rested body are your best chance at assessing a situation and responding with skill. Relentless self-interrogation, fault finding, and shame will not get you there.

Imagine the Best Thing Possible

Oh great, you might think, *now I have to be anxious about how anxious my thoughts are because thinking about disaster is making everything worse, and it's more likely to make me less skilled in the event of another emergency.*

Yeah. That's anxiety. It just keeps building on itself.

We've also got that pervasive cultural belief that your thoughts create your reality. A lot of our self-help books and false gurus tell us this, too—that if we were only more aware of our surroundings, if we were more attuned to *detail*, we'd not get into horrible situations. And if we're having a hard time, it's because we caused it somehow. With our thoughts. So there's a lot of cultural support for anxiety: you get what you think of, so you'd better be sure you're thinking the right thoughts. It's your own fault if something goes wrong.

"You create your own reality" is so patently untrue, and so cruel to the grieving heart. Many of us already feel responsible for what's happened, both the death of someone we love, and the fact that we somehow aren't doing our grief "well enough." While this adage might (and I mean might) have a bare thread of truth in it, for the most part, it's utter junk. Your thoughts can influence how you *respond* to what is, but your thoughts do not create what is.

You are many things, but you are not that powerful. You cannot manifest death or health or loss or grief just by thinking about it. Your thoughts did not create this loss. Your continued anxiety will not make more loss happen. Not being anxious and on guard will not "doom" you to more loss, nor will it protect you from harm.

If thinking could keep people safe, none of us would be grieving. If thoughts alone could prevent illness, accidents, and suffering, we would not have any of these. Magical thinking doesn't control reality.

What your thoughts *will* do is influence how you feel about yourself and about the world around you. The best way to work with your thoughts is to harness your amazing powers of imagination—evident in all those imagined disaster scenarios—in voting for the future you actually want, not the one you don't. Basically, I want you to use your brain's native powers for good, not for anxiety. If you must imagine something, please try imagining the best possible outcome. Let that be your guiding image. Not because it's going to affect anything (in either direction) but because it makes living here easier on you, and I want this easier on you.

If you're scared, and maybe waiting to see how something will unfold, *you* get to decide how you imagine the whole scene going. Given that nothing has happened yet, use your brain to imagine something beautiful.

Let your thoughts create an internal state of calm, and hopeful (if mild) optimism. That's the reality your thoughts can change.

Find the Middle Ground

The key to managing, or even transforming, anxiety is not in finding a place of safety, but in finding a place of neutrality. We all need reassurance. We all need a sense of safety, and life itself is inherently not "safe." The next moment could bring any number of things, some glorious, some horrendous. The only way I've found to live inside that reality is to tell myself that, currently, I'm not safe, and I'm not in danger either. Every moment is neutral.

That neutrality is what Eastern traditions, and some earlier Western traditions, are talking about when they speak of "nonattachment," or the calm, clear center. It's a space of alert calm: neither rehearsing disaster nor falling back into a denial of life's risks.

In any moment, something bad and something good are equally possible. Peace-of-being is in what we train ourselves to expect. In early grief especially, it may become a process and practice of choosing to believe in a benign moment. Not good, not bad. Not safe, not in danger. Right here, now, in this moment, you are . . . neutral. Those spaces in between, where you can breathe, where there is space—those are the places you want. This is what the ancient teaching practices are about: living in that neutral spot. Which is not at all the same as having equanimity "no matter what," or about being "above" everything somehow. It's about seeing the current situation, the current environment, for exactly what it is, without embellishment or future fantasy. To paraphrase Eckhart Tolle: Anxiety is using your imagination to create a future you do not want. So let's not do that.

If you can't believe in "safety," aim yourself toward neutral. It's a much more stable place than fear.

THE BIGGER ANSWER TO ANXIETY: WHAT, EXACTLY, DO YOU NEED?

We have so much shame around anxiety; we often pretend we aren't feeling it. It's never effective to pretend you aren't afraid. Pretending you aren't afraid makes your interpersonal relationships come out wonky and makes you feel incredibly unstable. Hiding your anxiety makes it shoot out sideways: you *act out* of your anxiety rather than *respond* to it.

Again we come back to acknowledgment as the most powerful medicine we have. It may seem counterintuitive, but somehow telling the truth: "I don't feel safe in the world right now," or "I'm afraid my dog will die," makes things different. Anxiety changes. It softens. Your grip on the outside world relaxes a little bit.

Telling the truth allows you to relax enough to ask yourself what you need in that moment. When you catch yourself imagining disaster scenarios, tell yourself the truth: "I am afraid of more loss." Lengthen your exhale. Ask yourself what you're truly looking for: What do you need in this moment? Possible answers to that question might be: reassurance, comfort, attachment, a nap—anything that establishes a truer sense of safety, not a situational one.

If you identify a need of, say, assurance or connection, what other ways might you answer those needs rather than rehearse un-winnable disasters or relentlessly check in about the safety of people you love? You might need more information about a situation, or you might need to actually ask for comfort or connection, rather than manage your fear of losing it.

If you're out somewhere, feeling scared about imagined threats to your child's or pet's safety, maybe you need to head home in order to care for yourself, rather than ignore your anxiety and attempt to push through. That's another form of self-kindness. Remember that anxiety is often made worse by lack of food or sleep; you might see it as a signal to care for your physical self.

As with most things, there is no one right answer. The important thing is to let yourself ask, "What do I need right now, and how can I best meet that need?"

You won't always get what you need. But the practice of asking yourself what you need, and taking the most likely-to-be-effective course of action to meet those needs, actually *builds* a sense of safety in the world. As a longer-term approach to anxiety, telling the truth and asking yourself what you need is highly effective. It works where other things cannot.

The phrase "It's better to put shoes on your feet than to cover the whole world in leather" is what I'm talking about. Safety does not live in the world around you. You can't control things enough to guard against loss. Safety resides solely in self-advocacy, listening to your own needs below the surface of your fears, and responding accordingly. You cannot prevent loss. Your "safety" resides in your own heart, in how you care for yourself, in how you imagine the world.

Please come to yourself—especially the anxious, fearful, terrified parts—with love and respect. This kind of anxiety is normal. It's yet another way your mind is trying to reorder the world after your loss. Your mind is trying to keep you safe. Do your best to soothe your hardworking, overworking mind when you can. Tell yourself the truth about your fears. Ask. Listen. Respond. Commit to caring for yourself inside whatever comes. Above all, be *kind* to yourself. As author Sharon Salzberg is known to say, "You yourself, as much as anybody in the entire universe, deserve your love and affection."

ANXIETY MAP

Are there patterns to my anxiety? When
is it more noticeable? What are my early
warning signs of exhaustion that may lead
to more anxiety?

If you aren't sure what sets off anxiety, you
might start logging the circumstances or
situations that make your anxiety worse.
Just as important, take note of what's been
happening on days where your anxiety is
lessened, or nonexistent. What's different
on those days?

When you feel anxious about a specific
situation, ask yourself what the actual
need is under the fear. Most often, there
is a need for connection, reassurance, or
stability. What needs do you identify?
What are some more effective ways to
get those needs met?

What would kindness to self look like in
response to your anxiety?

11

WHAT DOES ART HAVE TO DO WITH ANYTHING?

I want to tell you that the creative process will be healing for you, in and of itself. But I'm a terrible liar.

I can't bring up the creative process without being honest about my own path. The arts, or any artistic practices, were hard for me in the early days of grief. I resented words and writing for a really long time. I resented any creative process for a really long time. Even as I needed them.

I've been a writer all my life, and a visual artist, too. Because I had both art and writing as parts of my professional life before I became widowed, I heard several times how *lucky* I was: Lucky because I could write and make art from my experience. Lucky because I could turn this death around and make it a gift for others.

As though this loss, *my partner's sudden death*, were redeemed somehow by the act of writing about it or by making art from it. As though our life, *his life*, was a fair trade for whatever work came out of it.

There's a deep cultural presumption that creating something out of grief somehow makes it all even out in the end: That your deepest call is to transform your grief into a work of art that touches others. That when you do that, when you turn to creative expression in the depths of pain, you are, in fact, healing your grief. Creativity is a way to transform pain. The results of your creativity, if they're good enough, can help others transform their pain. It all works out. At the very least, art and writing will make you feel better, and you can get to "acceptance" of this loss faster.

That presumption does such a disservice, both to the creative practice and to you.

We need art. We need to create. It's part of being human. It's still a huge part of my life, and I don't want a life without it. A lot of my work draws on creative practices inside grief, so clearly, I haven't abandoned it. But when creative practice is pitched as a cure for grief, or as a necessary shattering in order to be of use, that's when I bristle, grind my teeth, start snarling.

Creating something good out of loss is not a trade, and it's not a cure.

Pain is not redeemed by art. Creating something out of what was is no fair trade for not being allowed to continue *living* what was. There is no fair trade. Whatever you might create in your pain, out of your pain, no matter how beautiful or useful it might be, it will never erase your loss. Being creative won't solve anything. Art is not meant to make things "right."

So this is tricky territory, both out in the world, and in this chapter on creative practices inside grief.

> There's a secret to this. My written words draw you closer. It's a seductive dance on a whole other level. It makes me think of Rumi's love poetry, which is really about his relationship with the Unknown. Love is clarified, drawn through a veil of language and distilled into something that is

closer to the divine. That's the best secret, my
writing draws you closer. . . . I am clothing you
with language, and you become more visible.

CHRIS GLOIN, Writing Your Grief student,
on the death of her husband, Bill

WHY DO IT THEN?

If we don't use creative practices to make grief better, why do
them at all? We engage in creative practices because our minds
(and our hearts) run on them.

Pain, like love, needs expression. The human mind naturally goes to creative expression: it's the way we're built. We
are storytelling creatures. We look to art, and to story, to help
us make sense of the world, especially when what's happened
makes no sense. We need images to live into, stories to guide us
in the new life that has come. We need the creative process to
bear witness to our own reality—to reflect our own pain back
to us. In a world that so often doesn't want to hear your pain,
the page or the canvas or the sketch pad is always a willing
companion.

When we separate the creative process from a need to solve
or fix things, it becomes an ally. It becomes a way to withstand grief, a way to reduce suffering, even as it can't change
the pain.

Creative practices can also help you deepen your connection with that which is lost. Death doesn't end a relationship;
it changes it. Writing, painting, and other creative processes
allow the conversation that began in life *Before* to continue in
life *After.* The stories we create are a continuation of love.

And sometimes, creation allows us to connect and relate to
the world again, in our own new ways, in this whole new life.

> I don't usually put into words the ache in my throat, the knot in my stomach, the headache that I get from holding back tears. Words have limits, but pain doesn't seem to. So what's the point? Words are imperfect tools. They can and do let us down often. But at their best, words can build a connection between me and another person, and it's that connection that matters to me. When you're connected to someone, when they get you, they know that the words you speak are only the tip of a huge iceberg of feelings, regrets, dreams, and memories. I built a bridge with Seth over thirty-five years; it was a work of art. It takes more courage than I realized to risk starting over, building bridges again, with other people. The cynical part of me tells me to get over the idea that words can console me, empower me, connect me. But the part of me that daydreams and hopes and tells stories carries on, uncertainly, toward the bridge.
>
> KATHI THOMAS ROSEN, Writing Your Grief student, on the death of her husband, Seth

While it's not pain's only role, pain often does call us into communication, even communion, with others. Without that call to express great pain, we wouldn't have images from Käthe Kollwitz. We wouldn't have Picasso's *Guernica*. We wouldn't get to feel our own pain reflected in the words of C. S. Lewis, or Cheryl Strayed, or Claire Bidwell Smith, or Emily Rapp. We take comfort from the company of our own kind, the people living deep loss alongside us, throughout time.

Creative practices are a balm, and a support, inside what can barely be endured. So while the creative practices in this chapter won't fix you, and can't bring back what you've lost, they can help you find a way to live what has been asked of you. They can help you tell the story of what is, in a way that makes things even just a tiny bit easier on both your mind and your heart. They can help you stay connected to who you've lost. They can help you connect to your companions inside grief. They can make things better, even when they can't make them right.

> At its best, the sensation of writing is that of any unmerited grace. It is handed to you, but only if you look for it. You search, you break your heart, your back, your brain, and then—and only then—it is handed to you.
>
> ANNIE DILLARD, *The Writing Life*

ON WRITING

Recent studies show that engaging in as little as ten to fifteen minutes of creative writing can help reduce overall levels of cortisol, the "stress hormone," in the body. While the studies say other things about emotional regulation, increasing optimism, and decreasing hostility, I think the safest corollary is that writing, in its effect on stress in the body, can help your physical organism survive this loss. As I said in chapter 9 on grief and the mind, tending your body makes grief, itself, easier to bear.

And it's not just the physiological effects that interest me. Any creative practice, including writing, can help reduce your suffering by allowing you to tell your own story.

Honestly, I can't tell you why writing helps. When Matt died, I quit almost everything—except writing. I wasn't writing to heal. I wasn't writing to communicate to others. I wasn't writing to find peace or resolution or acceptance. I was writing because I had to. Because words leaked out of me, whether I had paper in front of me or not.

In those early days, writing was how I connected with Matt, how I continued our conversation that was so abruptly stopped. It was how I recorded rare moments of calm, of feeling loved and grounded, places I could go back to and relive when everything had gone too dark to be endured. It was where I recorded those dark moments, too. On the page, everything is allowed. Everything has a voice.

In a podcast recently, I heard the speaker say something along the lines of writers live everything twice: once when it actually happens, and then again when they put it on the page. Writing this book, I've looked back on all those boxes and boxes of journals I wrote in the early days of grief. In them, I have a map of who I was back then, a series of entry points into the intensity of love and pain that marked those days. So writing can do that, too—it gives you a map. A topography of grief and love, a through-line to follow, should you ever need to return.

 In losing Coll, I've noticed that my normal coping mechanisms of achieving the peace that is brought on from the release of intense emotions haven't worked. When I cry, I don't feel better. When I yell and scream in an empty house, I don't feel better. Many times when I speak to my therapist, I do not feel better.

But writing—writing hasn't failed me. Writing has been healing when all else has failed. The edges of my emotions are still fairly jagged and raw, but they have been sanded down so they don't cut as deep with every breath. And that's all thanks to writing.

JENNY SELLERS, Writing Your Grief student, on the death of her partner, Coll

WRITING THE TRUTH (ALONE, TOGETHER)

Almost since the beginning of Refuge in Grief, I've run writing courses for grieving people. I never promise that writing will make anyone feel better. On the contrary, I ask my students to dive fully into their pain. Nothing is off-limits; nothing is too harsh.

When I ask my students how writing has helped them in their grief, without fail, they say that writing the true reality of their loss has helped them survive. We have such censorship around grief—in the larger world, certainly, but even in our own hearts and minds. We've been so well conditioned to not say what hurts. There's a freedom in letting all your words out. There is freedom in being heard. On the page, everything is welcome.

> Writing may not fix grief, but it may have given me the most important tool I have to live with it: a means to express the agony I've carried for fifteen years and a tribe of fierce and beautiful souls that not only honor that expression, but who also aren't afraid of it. They aren't afraid of it. By extension, they aren't afraid of me. Writing can't fix what happened. It can't undo what was done, rewrite history, or bring back my dead brother. It doesn't erase the pain, dull the grief, or make any of it suddenly "OK."
>
> Writing didn't fix me. It let me begin to honor myself, my own experience, and my own broken heart. My mantra through this time has been "The only way through is through." Through is what writing about my grief has given me. A tool to use to get through. Healing happened here. What a gift it is that no matter how heavy my words, they never, ever turn away.
>
> GRACE, Writing Your Grief student, on the death of her brother

My students have shown me, over and over again, the power in simply telling your own story, as it is. Your writing doesn't have to be good. It doesn't have to be "right." Through writing, grief and love, horror and companionship weave themselves into this story of your life—the true story. You can write for yourself alone, or you can find places to share your words with others. What matters most is telling the truth, without censure, without apology.

Words may be small, but they contain your heart, and your heart is always welcome to speak on the page.

GIVE GRIEF A VOICE

Even if you don't identify yourself as a writer, please give writing a try. Throughout this book, you'll find writing exercises and prompts to get you started; there's also a prompt included below. Set a timer for ten minutes. Even if you have to write the prompt itself, or write "Why am I doing this?" over and over, keep writing until the timer goes off. Once you've finished, draw (or type) a line under your writing. Below the line, write a few sentences about what it felt like to write your response to the prompt.[1] If your grief isn't "fixed" (spoiler: it won't be), is anything different? What did you find in your writing?

This prompt is taken from the Writing Your Grief course. I asked my students to nominate their favorites, and this one was the clear winner:

If you were writing fiction, you'd want to know the voice of your main character. You'd want to know the way they walk, the kinds of food they eat, how they comb or don't comb their hair. They would need to be *real*. In a way, your grief is a character: it has a rhythm and a voice. It is particular to you. If we're going to be working with grief, let's find out who it is.

The creative tool is called *personification*. What we're really doing is giving grief, itself, a voice. When it has a voice, it can tell us things. Let's think of this exercise as inviting your grief to introduce himself or herself to you. Here's an off-the-cuff example:

> Grief rocks, slumped in a corner, spent drink in her left hand, dirt smeared across her forehead.
>
> She hums and she cries; her hands flit against things I don't see. As I come near, she looks up, startled but clear-eyed:
>
> "What do you want?" she asks, adjusting the straps of her dress.
>
> She pats herself down gently.
>
> "What is it you most want? Maybe I have it. Maybe I have it somewhere . . ."

If your grief is a character who can come forward and speak, what kind of voice does it have? Don't tell us about it; let them actually speak. Write in grief's voice. To get there, you might begin by taking just a few moments to quiet yourself. Close your eyes. Take a few breaths. As you feel yourself center, pick up your pen or set your hands over the keyboard. Take another breath, and on the exhale, imagine you ask your pain this question:

"Who are you?" or *"Tell me who you are . . ."*

"

My words don't fade; they won't. I'll form a stronger rock, a sculptural force from which I will continue to build myself, a mother without her child. I will. I will shape my words with soft taps from my mothering mallet. I will carve these deep troughs of love into my life.

The powerful lyrics of death were unknown to me "before," though I sing them as mother tongue now. My words. Utterly heartfelt expressions of love for my son. My dead son. My son who died before I gave birth. These are my words. This is my truth. My son died. He is dead, and I love him. I've learned a new vocabulary.

CARLY, Writing Your Grief student,
on the death of her son, Zephyr

MORE THAN WORDS: GRAPHIC NOVELS

Matt was in incredibly good physical shape. This led my mother to suggest I write a comic book about him, a graphic novel, entitled *Mr. Universe*. It could follow his adventures beyond this earthly plane, out there in the galaxies somewhere, flying around . . . doing things.

Now, that kind of narrative is not my style. However, she had a point. The graphic novel has some fantastic creative elements. It's not a format I've played with, but it's definitely on my list. A graphic novel with an incredibly dark storyline sounds wonderful to me.

There are a number of examples out there if you'd like to explore this medium with some guidance. Writer and artist Anders Nilsen's books *Don't Go Where I Can't Follow* and *The End* follow his fiancé's, Cheryl's, illness and death, and his life after these events. *Rosalie Lightning: A Graphic Memoir* is a graphic novel written by Tom Hart on the sudden death of his two-year-old daughter, Rosalie. One of my favorite grief books, Michael Rosen's *The Sad Book*, illustrated by Quentin Blake, doesn't make sadness pretty, or cast loss in a romantic, it-works-out light. It is, simply, a book of Rosen's heart after the sudden death of his eighteen-year-old son, Eddie.

Even if you don't go full-on graphic novel, maintaining a sketchbook is a great practice. Sometimes, pictures and gesture drawings are far more accurate than words can ever be. Whatever your medium, don't be afraid to be as dark as you are. This is your life—your creative practice gets to reflect that, in fact, *should* reflect that.

COLLAGE

Sometimes, I simply cannot handle words. This was true before Matt died, and is even more true since. Words can be so vexing. Language can be so small. Although writing is a creative practice, it does still use parts of the mind used for logic and reason, and logic and reason simply do not play well with deep grief.

In my early grief days, there were times I stabbed through my journals, frustrated with the constraint of words. Frustrated that words were what I had left of our life. Enraged that I was supposed to fit this impossibility into syllables and sentences. Stupid, stupid words.

As an antidote to my word-heavy mind, I often went back to my old practice of making collages. There was something really satisfying about tearing apart magazines, destroying words and images and making them into something new, something mine. Much like the found poetry we'll talk about next, using other people's images to create a new narrative is deeply satisfying. I still do this. When I'm really into it, I do a collage a day, keeping them in a small art-paper sketchbook. Doing it as a daily practice helps me understand where I am, how I'm feeling, and lets me put things on the page that I simply do not care to write. And because I'm borrowing other people's images, I don't have to start from scratch.

As a daily check-in, making a collage is a fantastic practice: no words, no thought. You can use your collage practice as a way to check in with yourself, a way to center yourself inside the swirl of grief. It's a way to acknowledge what is real, what is true in this moment, no matter what this moment holds.

COLLAGE

TRY THIS

Gather a bunch of magazines and newspapers, decent scissors, glue sticks or other adhesive, and heavy sketch paper. I prefer shiny-paper magazines, the ones with more photos than text. There's no reason to buy them: look on Craigslist for someone giving away magazines rather than throwing them out, or check recycling boxes during an early morning walk around your neighborhood. There's never a shortage of magazines. I prefer small sewing-type scissors for this, as the cut work can get pretty tiny. Use heavy paper rather than thin, printer-type paper; that stuff will buckle and get wavy with the weight of glue and paper. You might even get a sketchbook specifically for this purpose.

Flip through your magazines, pulling out any image that calls you. Let your mind wander through the pages. It's normal to get caught up in an article from time to time, but do your best to drag yourself out of the narrative and focus on the photos.

You might look for larger images that can serve as a background, and several smaller images that you just like. Or find images you feel repelled by but cut out anyway. None of this has to make "sense." None of this has to be "art." Tear or cut out whatever you'd like. Once you've got a good assortment, start arranging and rearranging them on the paper. When you have the basic background and larger images where you'd like them, start gluing.

Remember, this isn't about making sense of anything or making something pretty. The images themselves will often dictate what the final form will be. If you find yourself getting too fiddly and perfectionistic, try setting a timer; knowing you need to finish soon can help you make decisions in a looser, more impulsive way. In collage work, impulsive = good.

FOUND POETRY

If you'd rather stick with words, or would like to add words to your collage practice, found poetry is a great collage-like tool.

FOUND POETRY

Find a newspaper, or any printed something—a book, flyer, catalog. Online text doesn't work as well. Open the paper to a full spread, one with lots of articles and words, not a bunch of photos. Get yourself a highlighter or colored pen. Close your eyes for a moment, take a good deep breath (as deep as you can). Exhale, and begin to lightly scan the paper, underlining random words from all over the page.

Let the available words dictate what is written, but don't feel stuck to one article or column. You can ramble all over. When you feel finished, write down the words and phrases you've underlined. You can rearrange the words, or leave them in the order they were found. Try it a few times; you'll be surprised by what you find.

There is no "topic" for this. In fact, if you're feeling overwhelmed or burned out on grief, make a ridiculous found-word story. Use different colors for different stories, or turn to a whole different section of the paper. Play with it. See what you find. You might even add your found poetry to your photo collage work: finish your collage, then search for a found poem to write the story of the visual image.

As with everything, please consider these to be experiments. Does creating an image or word-based collage change or shift something in you? Do you have even the tiniest breathing room as you do this? Does it soothe your rabid mind, if only for a time? Some people simply feel softer, or less tense, after these practices.

Much like the wellness-worseness exercise in chapter 7, messing around with collage and other processes can give you information about how you might carry your loss, or how you might live here with as much kindness to self as you can. Or maybe, as I often say, things like this don't do anything positive at all, but they do suck less than other things. Sometimes, that's your best metric: this sucks less than most things do. If you must do something, or you're driving yourself nuts with overthinking, borrow someone else's words or images for a while.

PHOTOGRAPHY, SCULPTURE, MACRAMÉ, AND THE CULINARY ARTS

There are a million different ways to be creative. I've focused mainly on writing and drawing here, but whatever feels right to you, that's the thing to do. I used to be a sculptor. I think working with clay is one of the most creative, cathartic, and healing activities there is. Many of my widowed friends turned to photography after their partners died. Some dove into knitting or other fiber arts. At least one person poured her creative energy into food, creating beautiful things to feed others in her life when her chosen family no longer had need to eat.

Whatever you do in your grief, please remember that it's yours. No one has the right to dictate what your art should look like, or that it should make you feel better. Creative exploration is a companion inside your grief, not a solution. As a mirror of your own innermost heart, let it be whatever it needs to be.

WORKS IN PROGRESS

All creative practices can help you see your life, see your heart, for what it is now. For some, especially those outside your grief, that might sound like a terrible thing. But really, hearing your own self speak, seeing your true reality out there, on the page—in writing, in painting, in photographs—shifts something.

> That first year, my grief-year, I could hardly believe what had happened. I carried my story outside of me, like a heavy, sharp, awkward object. It was impossible and ungainly, always scratching at my hands or dropping with an ugly thud on my big toe. I lugged that tale through the heat of summer, the colors of autumn, the snows of winter, and the rebirth of spring before I made enough space for it inside of myself.
>
> It's not a puzzle, you know. No amount of shoving can make that huge pointy weight fit into a neat little empty space, and no amount of turning could fit back together the pieces of my shattered heart. I had to learn to see it as a sculpting project, working the clay of my loss and the clay of myself until I could build something new from it, then, standing back, accept the work-in-progress as me.
>
> KATE CARSON, Writing Your Grief student,
> on the death of her daughter, Laurel

Your life, and your grief, are a work in progress. There is no need to be finished. There is no need to be perfect. There is only you, and the story of the love—and the loss—that brought you here. Find ways to tell your story.

12

FIND YOUR OWN IMAGE OF "RECOVERY"

Talking with people in new grief is tricky. During the first year, it's so tempting to say that things get better. I mean, is it really a kindness to say, "Actually, year two is often far harder than year one"? But if we don't say anything, people enter years two and three and four thinking they should be "better" by now. And that is patently untrue: subsequent years *can* actually be more difficult.

Then again, if we only talk about the deep realities of grief—the way it lingers and stays and sets up camp—then people have no hope. You can't just say, "Yes, this is horrible and awful, and it will be for a long time," without offering some kind of light in the distance.

We need a way to talk about both things—the reality of deep, persistent pain *and* the reality of living with that pain in a way that is gentle, authentic, and even beautiful. To do this, we need to talk about the words we use, and how we mean them.

> And now there is this, what has come after the death, after the sorrow: a softer loss. Not a

churning in my gut, but a settling of stones. I
sleep softer, and when that is elusive, I don't
fight it. I am still learning about this other side
of sorrow and loss. Where I ended and my grief
began is no longer a place. My sorrow and I
are the same, there is no separation. The Great
Divide that cracked opened when he died, it's a
crevice that runs deep, but it has a bottom that
curves up toward my future. It is a gash that I fill
with our love, a scar that I wear on my soul. I'm
incredulous, when I think of it, how this thing
came into me and found a place to live. I wish I
could tell him about it, how I carry him now.

MICHELE SACCO DWYER, Writing Your Grief student,
on the death of her husband, Dennis

YOU CAN'T RECOVER FROM "DEAD"

I am super particular about language. The wrong word choice
grates on me, even in the best of times. So when I was first
widowed, hearing words like *recovery* and *better* really bothered
me. Getting better sounded ridiculous. Exactly what was going
to improve?

How can you get better when the one you love is still dead?

Honestly. A loss of this magnitude is not something you
simply *recover* from.

Recovery, as defined in the dictionary, means to restore
oneself to a normal state, to regain what was lost, or to be
compensated for what was taken. I hear from a lot of people
grieving the loss of a child, or grieving the loss of their best
friend, sibling, or partner, grieving someone who should have
had twenty, thirty, eighty more years. I hear from people who
became paralyzed in accidents, or who survived large-scale acts

of violence. The whole idea of recovery is just plain strange in this kind of grief.

That hole torn in the universe will not just close back up so that you can go back to *normal*. No matter what happens next in your life, it will never be adequate compensation. The life you lost can't come back. That loss can't be regained.

By definition then, there is absolutely no point in time when you will "recover" from such a loss.

And that makes it tricky. If there is no "healing" in terms of being as good as new, if we can't "recover" any more than someone who has lost their legs can simply will them to grow back, how do we go on?

In order to live well with grief—in order to live alongside grief—I think we need new terms.

> I don't want time to heal me. There's a reason I'm like this.
> I want time to set me ugly and knotted with loss of you.
> CHINA MIÉVILLE, *The Scar*

THERE'S NO SUCH THING AS "MOVING ON"

We are changed by things that happen in our lives. This is always true. That we should be expected—even required—to return to normal after a devastating loss is even crazier when we realize that there is no such expectation in any other major life experience. As I've stated earlier, that insistence on returning to normal says far more about the speaker's discomfort with pain than it does about the reality of grief.

You will not "move on." You will not return to "who you used to be." How could you? To refuse to be changed by something as powerful as this would be the epitome of arrogance.

I love what researcher and author Samira Thomas has to say about this in terms of "resilience" and returning to normal:

There are some events that happen in life that cause people to cross a threshold that forever changes them, whether they seek out their transformation or not. Life is ever unfolding, and people are ever in a process of becoming. Resilience holds the etymological implications of resistance to crossing thresholds, and instead adapting an old self to new circumstances without offering space or time to be completely changed by new realities.

Unlike resilience, which implies returning to an original shape, patience suggests change and allows the possibility of transformation . . . It is a simultaneous act of defiance and tenderness, a complex existence that gently breaks barriers. In patience, a person exists at the edge of becoming. With an abundance of time, people are allowed space to be undefined, neither bending nor broken, but instead, transfigured.

SAMIRA THOMAS, "In Praise of Patience"[1]

We are changed by our new realities. We exist at the edge of becoming. We don't recover. We don't move on. We don't return to normal. That is an impossible request.

A dear friend of mine spent a good part of his early life working in mine restoration—the environmental practice that attempts to heal landscapes polluted and destroyed by intensive mining operations. This is such an intense—and often failing—prospect that many environmentalists have written off the restoration of mine sites. They are simply too damaged to be restored. My friend worked with, at the time, the only person who had found a way to restore these sites. It involved collaboration with native tribes, research into mineral and biological needs of various landscapes, and patient study of the land itself—watching the wounds, using them to inform the ecological changes moving forward. The work itself is intensive, backbreaking labor. It takes decades to see the results: flourishing ecosystems, the return of native plant and animal species, a landscape healed.

My friend says that people visiting these restored sites see only the beauty there. There is no obvious evidence of the destruction that came before. But for those who did the work, for those who saw what lies beneath all that new growth, those wounds are clearly evident. There are whole lifetimes buried beneath what now appears so beautiful. We walk on the skin of ruins.

The earth does heal—and so does the heart. And if you know how to look, you can always see the ravages underneath new growth. The effort and hard work and planning and struggle to make something entirely new—integrated and including the devastated landscape that came before—is always visible. That the devastation of your loss will always exist is not the same as saying you are "eternally broken." It is saying we are made of love and scars, of healing and grace, of patience. Of being changed, by each other, by the world, by life. Evidence of loss can always be seen, if we only know how to look.

The life that comes from this point on is built atop everything that came before: the destruction, the hopelessness, the life that was and might have been.

There is no going back. There is no moving on. There is only moving *with*: an integration of all that has come before, and all you have been asked to live. Samira Thomas continues, "From this landscape, I take the lesson that I need not be who I once was, that I may hold my scars and my joy simultaneously. I need not choose between bending or breaking but that, through patience, I may be transfigured."[2]

"Recovery" in grief is not about moving on. It's not about resilience or a return to "normal" life. Recovery is about listening to your wounds. Recovery is being honest about the state of your own devastation. It's about cultivating patience, not the kind that implies waiting it out until you return to normal, but patience in knowing that grief and loss will carve their way through you, changing you. Making their own kind of beauty, in their own ways.

Recovery inside grief is always a moving point of balance. There isn't any end point. While it may not always be this acutely heavy, your grief, like your love, will always be part of you. Life can be, and even likely will be, beautiful again. But that is a life built alongside loss, informed by beauty and grace as much as by devastation, not one that seeks to erase it.

If we talk about recovery from loss as a process of integration, of living alongside grief instead of overcoming it, then we can begin to talk about what might help you survive.

Given what cannot be restored, what cannot be made right, how do we live here? That's the real work of grief recovery—finding ways to live alongside your loss, building a life around the edges of what will always be a vacancy.

BUT WAIT—I DON'T WANT TO GET *BETTER*

I remember the first time I truly laughed after Matt died. I was horrified. How could I forget him, even for an instant? How could I find anything funny? It felt like a betrayal, not so much of Matt but of myself.

The whole idea of getting better—or even integrating your loss—can feel offensive, especially in early grief. Getting better might mean that the person you lost, or the life you no longer get to live, isn't as important anymore. For many people, their grief is their most vital connection to that which is lost. If happiness returns to your life, what does that mean about what was lost? Was it really not all that important, or special, if you can simply move forward with your life?

In my own early grief, I wasn't worried that I would always be in so much pain. I was worried that I one day wouldn't be. How could life possibly go on? And how could I live with myself if it did?

What I can tell you, several years down the road from my own loss, is that things get different; they don't get "better." In some ways, I do miss those early days. I miss being able to reach back and touch our life, miss finding his smell in the closet, being able to look in the refrigerator and see things he'd bought. Our life was so close to me then. And in that ripped-open state of early grief, love felt so close to me. It didn't fix anything, but it was there; it was present. There was no mistaking the power of that time, dark and painful as it was.

I don't miss the dry heaves, nightmares, distressing family politics, or the torn-open sense that there was nowhere left for me in the world. I look back at that earlier self, that earlier me, and, honestly, the pain I see there is incredibly hard to witness. While there are parts of those early days I almost even long for, that visceral pain is not something I miss.

That pain and my love for Matt were—and are—connected, but they aren't the same thing.

It is true that the pain you feel now is intimately connected to love. And—the pain will eventually recede, and love will stay right there. It will deepen and change as all relationships do. Not in the ways you wanted. Not in the ways you deserved. But in the way love does—of its own accord.

Your connection to that which you've lost will not fade. That's not our definition of *better*. As you move forward in this life, your grief, and more important, your love, will come with you. Recovery in grief is a process of moving *with* what was, what might have been, and what still remains.

None of this is easy.

Grief, like love, has its own timeline and its own growth curve. As with all natural processes, we don't have complete control over it. What is in your control, what is under your power, is how you care for yourself, what qualities of love and presence you bring to yourself, and how you live this life that has been asked of you.

HOW DO YOU "HOPE" INSIDE THIS?

As I mentioned at the start of this chapter, it's a particular challenge to talk about the realities of grief while also offering some kind of encouragement. When I talk about how difficult and long-lasting grief can be, outsiders often say, "But you have to have hope!"

By this time, it's probably not a surprise that I have issues with the use of the word *hope*. Whenever I read or hear somebody say, "You have to have hope," I always add, usually in my head, "Hope in what?"

Hope is a word that needs an object: you have to have hope *in something*.

Before a loss, many people "hoped" for a good outcome (for example, cancer remission or that their friend would be found alive and well) and can no longer believe in the power of hoping for anything.

Inside grief, some people "hope" that they'll survive whatever has erupted in their lives. They might hope to be happy again someday. Or they hope that their lives will get better from here on out, even better than they were before this loss happened.

Especially in my early grief, none of those definitions worked for me. Hoping for a better life just felt wrong. I loved my life. I loved who I was in my life. It felt wrong to think that Matt's death could make anything *better*. Hoping to be happy again felt like I was leaving part of myself behind.

I could not hope in survival, in improvement, or in happiness. The hopes I had at the riverside evaporated when his body was found.

That's the problem with hope. It's so often presented as end-goal focused: hope for how things will look, how things will turn out later. It's tied to a sense of control over the physical outcome of life: what you hope to *get*.

Insisting that we have hope in some kind of positive outcome is just another way our culture's insistence on transformation and a happy ending shows itself. I can't hope like that.

If we change our orientation to hope—moving from what we might get, to *how we might get there*—then hope is a concept I can get behind. We might not hope for a specific physical outcome, but instead hope to live this experience of loss in a way that is beautiful and personally meaningful.

There are so many ways to live inside this ever-changing relationship with grief, with love, with the person you lost, with yourself, and with life.

The most authentic hope I can offer you, or ask of you, is that you find ways to be true to yourself inside of this, inside all those changing things. I hope that you keep looking for beauty, hope that you find and nurture a desire to even *want* to look for it. I hope that you reach for your connection to love, that you seek it out as your anchor and your constant, even when all else has gone dark.

MOVING WITH: WHAT'S YOUR IMAGE OF RECOVERY?

There's a great book called *Elegant Choices, Healing Choices* by Dr. Marsha Sinetar. It outlines exactly the kind of hope I'm talking about: in any situation, we can reach for the most elegant, well-skilled, compassionate path. Wanting that for yourself, reaching for it, even if you don't always attain it, is, to me, the foundation of both hope and recovery inside loss.

Recovery is less about becoming "good as new," or even moving past your intense grief, and more about living this experience with as much skill, self-kindness, and peace-of-being as you can. Recovery takes patience, and a willingness to sit with your own heart, even, and especially, when that heart has been irrevocably shattered.

In your own ways, and in your own time, you will find ways to stitch this experience into your life. It will change you, yes. You may become more empathetic, as you know how the wrong words can cut, even when well-intentioned. It may also make you more short-tempered, with a severely shortened fuse for other people's cruelty or ignorance. In fact, that happens for a lot of people: in loss, we often become protective of others' pain, correcting and redirecting others who would inflict more pain by trying to take it away.

Grief changes you. Who you become remains to be seen. You do not need to leave your grief behind in order to live a newly beautiful life. It's part of you. Our aim is integration, not obliteration.

ON SOVEREIGNTY

Whether we call it recovery or integration or some other term, what's most important is that you choose this path for yourself.

With so much outside pressure to do something different in your grief—more of this, less of that, you should really try this, how about you start a foundation or run a marathon?—it can start to feel like your life is no longer your own. Everyone has an opinion. Everyone has an idea for how you might make meaning of this loss.

Before Matt died, and even more so now, sovereignty has been my personal bandwagon. Sovereignty is the state of having authority over your own life, making decisions based on your own knowledge of yourself, free of outside rule or domination. We're such an opinion-giving culture; it can be hard to remember that each person is an expert in their own life. Other people may have insight, yes, but the right to claim the *meaning* of your life belongs solely to you.

Because I am so sensitive to ideas of sovereignty and self-authority, any outside person telling me what my own recovery might look like is going to be met with irritation. But if I do the asking, if I wonder—*for myself*—what healing or recovery might look like, then it becomes a very different question.

It comes down to this: If you choose something for yourself, as a way of living this grief, it's perfect and beautiful. If something—even the very same thing—is foisted upon you by an outside force, it's probably not going to feel very good. The difference is in who claims it as the "correct" choice.

This is your life. You know yourself best. However you choose to live this life is the right choice. One of my teachers used to say, "It doesn't matter what choice you make; it matters that the choice be what is most true for you, based on who you know yourself to be."

Staying true to yourself, holding fiercely to your own heart, your own core—these are the things that will guide you.

MADE IN YOUR OWN IMAGE

It's important, especially in such a disorienting time, to give yourself an image to live into. Something to hope for. Something *yours*.

Remember, this isn't about improving you. You didn't need this loss. Recovery inside grief is entirely about finding those ways to stay true to yourself, to honor who you are, and what has come before, while living the days and years that remain. Recovery lies less in what you'll *do*, and more in how you'll approach your own heart, how you'll live this life that's asked of you.

If you are very, very new to this grief, this may not be the time to even wonder about healing. But if it feels right to gently question, asking yourself about your own recovery can be a genuine act of love and kindness.

IMAGINE RECOVERY

There are many ways to craft an image of your own recovery. To get started, you might write your responses to these questions:

Given that what I've lost cannot be restored, given that what was taken cannot be returned, what would healing look like?

If I step outside of the cultural norms of "rising above loss," what would *living this well* look like?

How will I care for myself?

What kind of person do I want to be, for myself, and for others?

While you can't know what events will happen in your life, you might wonder about how you want to *feel* inside your life. Do you hope for peace-of-being, or a sense of connection to self and others? What's the quality of heart and mind you'd like to cultivate? What can you reach for? What do you find hope in?

If you move your mind to the future, what does your grief look like? How have both love and loss been integrated? What does it feel like to carry this with you?

On a more practical level, what parts of early grief will you be glad to leave behind? Is there anything you can do, now, to help those parts soften or release?

You might write through your answers to create an overarching guide for this time in your life, or you might choose to ask yourself some of these questions on a daily basis, checking in with what might feel like recovery in this moment, on this day.

There certainly aren't easy answers to these questions. The answers themselves may change over time. But wondering about your own path forward is a gift you can give yourself. It starts when you ask yourself: If I can't *recover*, what would healing really be? What life do I want for myself?

If you need ideas of what recovery could look like, you might refer back to what you wrote in chapter 7: the wellness versus worseness exercise can give you clues.

■ ■ ■

Throughout this part of the book, I've tried to give you tools to use to reduce your suffering and tend your pain. Remember that grief itself is not a problem, and as such, cannot be fixed. Grief is a natural process; it has an intelligence all its own. It will shift and change on its own. When we support the natural process of grief, rather than try to push it or rush it or clean it up, it gets softer. Your job is to tend to yourself as best you can, leaning into whatever love, kindness, and companionship you can. It's an experiment. An experiment you were thrown into against your will, but an experiment all the same.

Keep coming back to the exercises and suggestions I've shared here. As you live forward in this loss, your needs will likely change. Revisiting these tools can keep you in touch with the ways your heart and mind shift inside your grief.

In the next part, we turn from the internal process of grief to our needs for community, support, and connection. It's in that wider community that we find both our deepest comfort and our largest disappointments. In telling the truth about how our support systems fail, we begin to create communities capable of bearing witness to pain that can't be fixed.

PART III

WHEN FRIENDS AND FAMILY DON'T **KNOW** WHAT TO DO

13

SHOULD YOU EDUCATE
OR IGNORE THEM?

If you're like most grieving people, the response from people around you has been clumsy at best, and insulting, dismissive, and rude at worst. We talked about the deep roots of pain avoidance and the culture of blame in earlier parts of this book. It's also important to bring it all back to your personal life, to help you understand—and correct—the unhelpful support of the people around you.

Being dismissed, cheered up, or encouraged to "get over it" is one of the biggest causes of suffering inside grief.

There's a catch-22 in grief support: because we don't talk about the realities of grief in our culture, no one really knows how to help. The people who can best tell us how to help—grieving people themselves—don't have the energy, interest, or capacity to teach anyone how to be supportive. So we're stuck: friends and family want to help, grieving people want to feel supported, but no one gets what they want.

If we're going to get better at supporting each other, if we're going to get what we all want—to love and be loved—we need to talk about what isn't working. It's not easy, but it's important.

" Showing up at my door ten days after my daughter died with a package of Pepperidge Farm smiley face cookies and telling me to smile, while you inanely grin at me, will not endear you to my broken heart. Expecting me to support you because the nature of our friendship has changed since my child has died is more than I can handle. When I tell you I am not up for big social gatherings (by *big* I mean more than one other person), please believe that I know what I can and cannot deal with. My instinctive need to cocoon, to swaddle myself in this horror is what I need to do right now. And I can't do that with you being all judgy over my shoulders, telling me I am angry all the time. Fuck, yes, I am angry! MY DAUGHTER IS DEAD! So come back later when you are willing to be silent and listen and watch.

And then there is this:

My tragedy is not contagious; you will not catch your children's death from me. I know you don't know what to say. I wouldn't have a few months ago, either. A little advice? Don't platitude me. Do not start any sentences with the phrase "at least," for you will then witness my miraculous transformation into Grief Warrior. I will spout grief theory at you, tell you that Kübler-Ross was misinterpreted, that there is no timeline, no road or path in grief. We are all on our own here, in the gloom. I will ask you to please talk about my daughter. That I am terrified that she will be forgotten, that I will somehow forget her. I will remind you that I

might tear up, or sob, but it's OK; this is my life
now. This is how I exist, in the here-and-not-now.

LAURIE KRUG, Writing Your Grief student,
on the death of her daughter, Kat

BUT I'M JUST TRYING TO HELP!

"Everything happens for a reason." What a ridiculous, shame-based, reductionist, horrible thing to say to anyone—let alone someone in pain. What reason could there possibly be?

"He had a great life, and you were lucky to have him for as long as you did. Be grateful, and move on." As though a great life lived makes it OK that that great life is now over.

"At least you know you can have a baby. I can't even get pregnant." When did the death of my baby turn into a story about your life?

"Cheer up! Things can't possibly be as bad as your expression makes them seem." Why do random strangers insist on telling me I should be happier?

The things we say to one another. The things we do, insisting that we're trying to help.

It's the most common, most universal, feedback I get from grieving people: the way they're treated in their grief is horrendous. People say the most incredibly insensitive and cruel things to people in pain. Sometimes they mean to. Sometimes people are mean and insensitive and cruel because that is who they are. Fortunately, those people are easier to ignore. But the ones who truly love you, the ones who desperately want to help? The things they say, the ways they entirely miss the pain you're in, they're much harder to deal with.

We know they mean well. We can see it on their faces, hear it in their voices: they want so badly to make this better. That they can't make it better just makes them try harder.

But you can't say that. You can't tell them they aren't helping. That just makes it worse.

JUST BE POLITE

When I talk about how badly we support people in pain, I get one of two responses: from grieving people, I hear "Thank you for saying this!" and from those outside others' pain I hear "We're only trying to help! Why are you so negative?"

The backlash is inevitable: "People mean well!" "They're only trying to help!" and even "You're clearly not evolved enough to hear the message underneath their words." The angriest letters I receive are from people trying their best to support someone they love, and here I am telling them that they're doing it wrong. Telling them that the words they use somehow *imply* hurtful, mean, dismissive things, when the very last thing they intend is to cause more harm. How can I be so heartless, so negative, so unable to see that they're doing their best? They mean well. I need to start looking for the good, be more grateful and more gracious, stop sounding so angry and mean.

Here's the thing: I tell the truth about what it's like to feel unsupported and dismissed inside grief. I tell the truth about how much we fail each other. I'm not afraid to say what grieving people all over the world think to themselves a million times every single day. I'm not afraid to say, out loud, "You are not helping."

I'm not being negative. I'm telling the truth.

We have a gag order on telling the truth. Not just the truth about grief, but the truth about how it feels to be a grieving person in our culture. We're trained to be polite. We're supposed to smile and nod and say, thanks for thinking of me, when inside, what we really want to do is scream, *"What the fuck are you thinking, saying that to me?"*

When I open a new community space for the writing course, I'm always struck by the number of people who say, "This is the first place I can be completely honest about my grief. No one else wants to hear about it, or they tell me I'm doing it wrong."

Many grieving people have told me that rather than tell people their words aren't helpful, they've chosen to stop speaking altogether. When you stop telling the truth because other people don't like it, that's a gigantic, unnecessary injustice on top of your pain.

No one likes to be told they're doing something wrong. But if we can't say what's true for us inside our grief, what's the point? If we can't say, "This doesn't help," without being shamed or corrected, how are people supposed to know what we need? If we don't say anything, if we instead smile and nod and excuse people because they "mean well," how will anything ever change?

Having your truth dismissed always feels bad. I didn't like it when it was done to me, and I hate it when it's done to you. I'm not immune to fits of anger when it comes to this.

Personally, I believe in what the mystics call "holy outrage"—the anger that fuels truth telling. It's the anger that points out injustice and silencing, not just to make a scene, but because it knows what true community *might* be.

Holy outrage means telling the truth, no matter who gets offended by the telling. And equally important, it means doing so in the service of more love, more support, more kinship, and true connection.

I spend so much time talking about the reality of unhelpful grief support because I want it to get better. I need it to get better. And so do you. So do the millions of people who will enter this grief world after us. It has to get better. So we have to start telling the truth.

It's not enough to say, "They mean well." It's not enough for someone to say they want to be of comfort, but insist on using words that feel dismissive or rude.

If someone truly wants to help you inside your grief, they have to be willing to hear what doesn't help. They have to be willing to feel the discomfort of not knowing what to say or how to say it. They have to be open to feedback. Otherwise they aren't really interested in helping—they're interested in being *seen* as helpful. There's a difference.

No one knows the right thing to say. That's why it's important to have these dialogues. Not so that we get it right, but so that we do it better.

DECIDING WHO WARRANTS CARE AND EFFORT

Educating people about the reality of grief is important—and sometimes you just don't have it in you to care if they get it or not. Sometimes it makes it easier on you if you simply stop trying to explain. At least stop trying to explain to most people. The trick is deciding who warrants your time and energy and who can be safely ignored. Once you've decided who deserves attention, the next step is helping them to help you—without adding more stress to your mind and heart.

None of this is easy.

If what I say here helps you educate and inform the kind-hearted, well-intentioned people in your life, great.

And if you can't find the energy to educate and inform, here: let me. Use this chapter, and the next (and the "How to Help a Grieving Friend" essay in the appendix), to help the people in your life understand, if even just a little more, what it's like to be living this grief. We can educate them, together.

ASSUMPTIONS. EVERYBODY'S GOT 'EM

How many times has someone come up to you and said, "You must feel so (fill in the blank)" or "I saw you standing there in line, thinking of your husband—I could tell by the way you looked off into space."

Or you find out, days or weeks after the fact, that someone's feelings were hurt when you didn't respond to them in a certain way, or that you didn't seem to want to talk to them. Meanwhile, you have no recollection of even seeing them at all.

Or people launch into long speeches about what you should do to fix your pain because this is what they did when (fill in the blank) happened to them. How stunningly odd that is, to hear that you might just need to go out dancing after your child dies because that's what the speaker needed after their divorce.

I remember how often people outside my grief would go on and on about my finding someone new, that my life would be great again one day, and that Matt would want these things for me. They would talk for such a long time, giving me pep talks, solving problems for me—problems that I hadn't articulated and wasn't actually experiencing.

So often in grief, we're told by people *outside our experience* what the experience is like for us: what it means, what it feels like, what it *should* feel like. They take their own experiences, their own guesses about what we're really wrestling with, and offer their support based on their own internal views. People take our social reactions—or nonreactions—personally, ascribing meaning to them without ever checking out their assumptions.

Making assumptions is normal. Everyone does it.

In our everyday lives, our own lived reality is usually far different from what others assume. In grief, that gulf between assumption and actuality is even wider. There is so much room for misunderstanding, and so little interest, or energy, in the griever to track down or correct those misunderstandings. It all adds to the exhausting experience of grief.

Just as in regular, non-grief times, there's likely a range of people in your life, from the truly kind and loving to the indifferent, self-absorbed, and strange. There are people who don't care one bit about your pain, and people who are far more concerned with being seen as helpful and important than they are in actually *being* helpful. Trauma and loss also bring out voyeuristic responses from some people, especially if your loss was made public with a "news" campaign.

All these people, even the great ones, are weird and awkward in the face of grief. They just show it in different ways.

It's tempting to write everyone off—no one gets it. No one understands. Living in grief can feel like you've moved to an entirely different planet, or make you wish you could.

It would be so great to be able to just transmit, without speaking, the reality of this loss in your life. To have people feel—just for thirty seconds—what it is you carry every second of every day. It would clear up so much misunderstanding. It would stop so much unhelpful "help" before it ever reached your ears. But we don't have that. We have words, and descriptions, and endless attempts to be understood and to understand.

The excessive, unrelenting need to describe your grief to someone, or correct their assumptions, just so they can support you better is one of those added cruelties inside grief.

TO SHARE OR NOT TO SHARE: HOW DO YOU TELL PEOPLE YOUR STORY?

In the early days after Matt died, I told everyone what happened. I couldn't help it. I cried easily, and often. People asked, and I told them. After a while, it felt weird and wrong, and too exposed, to give people this information. I got tired of the probing questions, the pitying looks, the hand placed softly on my forearm as a stranger leaned in to hear the details of my life.

And to be completely honest—not everyone deserved to have this most intimate information.

Do you have people in your life who don't deserve to know about your grief or who you've lost?

I'm talking about those people who don't handle the information with the skill and reverence and grace it deserves. I'm talking about the people who respond to this delicate information with the skill of a raging elephant—stomping around, asking questions, or worse, brushing it off like it was no big thing.

There are also just times when you want to keep your head down, get your groceries, walk the dog, and not feel you have to dive into your grief with every random person who stops you on the street to ask, "How are you *really*?"

Some people feel that they have to respond to every question about how they're doing, regardless of the actual relationship they have with the person asking.

Lots of people feel horrible if they don't mention the one they've lost, as if by not saying something, they're erasing the person, denying their central place in their lives. A lot of people feel awful when they sidestep and evade questions they'd rather not answer.

As with all other times in life, you do not have to do anything that goes against your own safety—whether that is physical or emotional.

If you choose to not reveal your inner life, your broken heart, or even the cold hard facts to other people, you are not betraying the one you've lost. Though it feels bizarre to talk around the gaping hole in your life, to answer, "I'm fine, thanks" to a routine question when you are not in any way fine really is a kindness to yourself. It *can* be a kindness to yourself.

Not everyone deserves to hear your grief. Not everyone is *capable* of hearing it. Just because someone is thoughtful enough to ask doesn't mean you are obliged to answer.

Part of living with grief is learning to discern who is safe and who is not, who is worthy and who is not. Part of living with grief is also learning to discern, for yourself, your own right timing in sharing this with others.

It's OK to be cautious about what you share and when. Your grief is not an open book, and it doesn't have to be. When, where, and with whom you share will shift and change over time, and sometimes even within the same day, but you always get to choose.

Those who support your shifting needs are the ones to keep in your life. The others? They can be set free.

"The baby died."

"Oh my god, I'm so sorry," she breathes. She is full of apologies, and I believe they are sincere. Yet she doesn't leave right away. "How did the baby die?" she asks.

A and I look at each other again. Is this woman for real? She expects us to relive the past forty-eight hours to satisfy her curiosity?

We answer her because we believe we must. Because we believe everything the hospital tells us. We endure all that happens to and around us, because we don't know any better. Because we are in shock. Because who comes prepared to deal with a dead baby?

It is not in our nature to be so rude as to say, "None of your goddamn fucking business." So we tell her. Cord accident. Short, clipped answers. Hoping she will stop. Hoping she will go away.

BURNING EYE, in her essay, "Milk," on Glow in the Woods

GRIEF REARRANGES YOUR ADDRESS BOOK

It's kind of a dorky statement, but it is true that grief rearranges your address book. It's amazing how many people drop out of your life in the wake of catastrophic loss. People who have been with you through thick and thin suddenly disappear, or turn dismissive, shaming, strange. Random strangers become your biggest, deepest source of comfort, if even only for a few moments.

It's one of the hardest aspects of grief—seeing who cannot be with you inside this. Some people fade out and disappear. Others are so clueless, so cruel (intentionally or not), you choose to fade out on them.

I dropped a lot of people in my life after Matt died. I simply could not tolerate them anymore: sudden, accidental death and its aftermath really highlights even the smallest relational mismatch. I gained a lot of people in my life—people whose skill and love surprised me, supported me, helped me survive. And a small handful of my dearest friends stayed beside me the entire time, through those brutal early days and beyond.

Grief can be incredibly lonely. Even when people show up and love you as best they can, they aren't really with you in this. They can't be. It so very much sucks that, in large part, you *are* in this alone. And also, you can't do this alone.

You may find that people come in and out of your life during this time. There are people who were instrumental in helping me survive those first few weeks who eventually moved back into their own lives, their own needs. They came into my life for a time, and then we let each other go. It hurt, that they had their own intact lives to get back to, but for a time, I was everything for them, and I knew it. Good people will show up as they can, for as long as they can. That they leave is not a failure, even though it hurts.

If there are people in your life you love, who love you, but this whole grief thing is making things a little clunky, it's OK.

Grief is difficult on everything; relationships are not immune. There will be people who can handle the choppy relationship bits and make it through with you. Hopefully the love and trust you've built together is resilient, giving you a net to fall into.

But not everyone will make it through this with you. Not everyone *should*.

It's true in all of life, but even more so inside grief: there is no time for relationships that make you feel small, shamed, or unsupported. This is your grief. Your loss. Your life. Honestly, this isn't really the time for relationship repair, or excessive social graces. It doesn't matter if some people *think* they're helping: if their form of support feels dismissive, judgmental, or just plain wrong, you do not have to keep them as friends.

If there are people in your life causing more harm than good, it's OK to cut them out. Your life is very different now, and some people simply do not fit.

For those who cannot make the transition with you into this new, unasked-for life, it's OK to bow to them, bow to the friendship you've shared, and let them go. It's not their fault. It's not yours. It's part of grief. Sometimes the best form of love is to let people go.

> Traumatized human beings recover in the context of relationships: with families, loved ones, AA meetings, veterans' organizations, religious communities, or professional therapists. The role of those relationships is to provide physical and emotional safety, including safety from feeling shamed, admonished, or judged, and to bolster the courage to tolerate, face, and process the reality of what has happened.
>
> BESSEL VAN DER KOLK, *The Body Keeps the Score: Brain, Mind, and Body in the Healing of Trauma*

STEP AWAY FROM THE MADNESS:
HOW TO STOP ARGUING ABOUT GRIEF

It really is a kindness to remove certain people from your life when you're in this much pain. But what about those people you can't cut out of your life, those permanent fixtures who are not supportive of you in any way? Those people who insist on cheering you up, or checking to see if you're over this yet? You can't always walk away from family members, or people you see consistently inside your chosen communities.

A newsletter reader sent me this question: "How can I deal with people who expect me to be 'over this' already? My fiancée died almost two years ago. How can I convince them it's all right that I'm not 'over it'?"

Though this question was sent by one reader, lots of people struggle with this issue. So many people expect you to be over it, if not already, then certainly in the very near future. They can't possibly understand what it's like to be you, to live inside grief like this. They want the "old" you back, not understanding that that old you can't come back. That self is gone.

It's so tempting, so easy, to be drawn into arguments, or to defend your right to your grief.

The thing is, no matter how much you say, no matter how much you try to educate them, they *can't* understand. As tempting as it is to give them that verbal smackdown (even nicely), your words aren't ever going to get through.

So what can you do?

Sometimes it just makes it easier on you, easier on your heart and mind, if you simply stop trying to explain.

■ ■ ■

Refusing to explain or defend your grief doesn't mean you let other people go on and on about it, continually telling you how you should live. I'm talking about stepping out of the argument altogether by simply refusing to engage in debates about whether or not your continued grief is *valid*.

Defending yourself against someone who cannot possibly understand is a waste of your time and your heart.

The important thing to remember is that your grief, like your love, belongs to you. No one has the right to dictate, judge, or dismiss what is yours to live.

That they don't have the right to judge doesn't stop them from doing it, however.

What that means is: If you want to stop *hearing* their judgment, you'll need to clarify your boundaries. You'll need to make it clear that your grief is not up for debate.

STEP AWAY

While it's certainly easier said than done, there are steps you can take to remove yourself from the debate:

1. Clearly and calmly address their concern.

2. Clarify your boundaries.

3. Redirect the conversation.

These three steps, when used consistently, can significantly reduce the amount of judgment that makes it to your ears. Here's how this might look in actual practice:

First, acknowledge their concern while presuming friendly intent: "I appreciate your interest in my life."

Second, clarify your boundaries: "I am going to live this the way that feels right to me, and I'm not interested in discussing it."

Steps one and two—addressing their concerns and clarifying your boundaries—often get combined in one statement: "I appreciate your interest in my life. I'm going to live this the way that feels right to me, and I'm not interested in discussing it."

This can be especially effective when you follow your statement with step number three, redirecting the conversation, aka changing the subject: "I'm happy to talk about something else, but this is not open for discussion."

It sounds wooden and strange, I know. But the message here—including the formal wording—is that you have a clear boundary, and you will not allow it to be breached in any way.

If there are people in your life who won't take such a clear boundary without further argument, you can stick to a stock phrase, "That isn't a topic I'll discuss," and then move the conversation on to something else.

If they can't do that, you can end the conversation completely—walk away, or say good-bye and hang up.

The important thing is to not allow yourself to be drawn into battle. Your grief is not an argument. It doesn't need to be defended.

It's awkward at first, but clarifying your boundaries and redirecting the conversation will become a lot easier the more you practice it.

Eventually, the people in your life will either get the message—not that you don't have to be over it, but that *you aren't willing to discuss it*—or they will leave. Even those people who seem immoveable and permanent will fall away if they have to.

The thing is, grief will absolutely rearrange your relationships. Some people will make it through, and some will fall away. Some people you thought would always be by your side will disappear entirely. People who were at the periphery of your life might step up and support you in ways you didn't see coming.

If the people in your life can handle, even appreciate, you staying true to your own heart, then they'll make it through with you. If they can't, let them go: gracefully, *clearly*, and with love.

14

RALLYING YOUR SUPPORT TEAM

Helping Them Help You

Our friends, our families, our therapists, our books, our cultural responses—they're all most useful, most loving and kind, when they help those in grief to carry their pain, and least helpful when they try to fix what isn't broken.

Most people want to help; they just don't know how.

There's such a huge gap between what people want for us, and what they actually provide with their support. It's no one's fault, really. The only way to close that gap is to let people know what works, what doesn't, and how we can all improve our skills in caring for each other.

Just because your grief can't be fixed doesn't mean there's nothing for your support teams to *do*. There are tangible, concrete ways to support people in grief. It just takes practice, and a willingness to love each other in new and different ways.

By shifting the focus away from fixing your grief onto actually supporting you *inside* it, friends and family can get that much closer to showing you the love they intend. They can make this better, even when they can't make it right.

I want you to be able to hand this book off to friends and family members who want to help you. I want you to direct them to the guidelines and suggestions in this chapter, so that you do not expend any of your energy in explaining your needs. The tools here will help them learn how to love you in this, how to come up alongside you, right inside your pain, without trying to cheer you up.

This chapter, more than any other, speaks to your support team rather than directly to you.

> When my friend Chris's young son died, I told her about how my therapist used to ask our group to "be like the elephants" and gather around the wounded member. I knew I couldn't really help her process the grief, but I could be there, at first just a body sitting close to her, later a voice on the phone. She told her friends about the elephants, and people started giving her little gifts or cards with elephants, just saying "I'm here." Gather your elephants, love. We are here.
>
> **GLORIA FLYNN, friend of the author, in a personal message**

SHIFTING FROM GRIEF AS A PROBLEM TO BE SOLVED TO AN EXPERIENCE NEEDING SUPPORT

If you're feeling frustrated and helpless in the face of someone's grief—you're normal. It's not your fault that you don't know what to do when you're faced with great pain in yourself or someone you love. Our models are broken.

We've got a medical model in Western culture that says that death is failure. We've got a psychological model that says anything other than a stable baseline of "happy" is an aberration. Illness, sadness, pain, death, grief—they're all seen as problems in need of solutions. How can you possibly be expected to handle grief with any skill when all of our models show the wrong approach?

Grief is not a problem. It doesn't need solutions.

Seeing grief as an experience that needs support, rather than solutions, changes everything.

It may seem like a small shift, just the change of a few words. Think of the space shuttle: two degrees difference on the ground translates into thousands of miles through space. The foundation you stand on as you approach grief influences everything—you will either get where you most truly wish to go (to love and support the people in your life), or you will fly wildly off course.

Let me give you an example. If you feel that grief is a problem, you will offer solutions: *You should get rid of her clothes. He's in a better place now, so try to be happy. You can't just sit around and be sad all the time; they wouldn't want that for you. Maybe you should get out more.*

You will encourage your grieving friend or loved one to do what you suggest because you're trying to relieve their pain—they have a problem, and you're doing your best to solve it. You get frustrated because your friend seems defensive. They don't want to take your advice.

The more you try to help—aka fix it—the more obstinate they become. Clearly, they don't want to get better.

The griever, on the other hand, knows that their grief is not something that can be fixed. They know there is nothing wrong with them. They don't have a "problem." The more people try to fix their grief, the more frustrated (and defensive) they feel. The griever is frustrated because they don't need solutions. They need support. Support to live what is happening. Support to carry what they are required to carry.

Grieving people expend a lot of energy defending their grief instead of feeling supported in their experience of it. Support people feel unwanted, unappreciated, and utterly helpless. This isn't working.

Even when you mean well, trying to fix grief is always going to turn out badly. This may be hard to hear, but if you truly want to be helpful and supportive, you need to stop thinking that grief is a problem to be solved.

When you shift to thinking of grief as an experience to be supported, loved, and witnessed, then we can *really* talk about what helps. When we stand on the same ground together, our words and actions can be truly supportive and useful.

The good news is that there are skills here. Just because there aren't *many* models of how to support someone doesn't mean there aren't *any*. There are things you can do—not to make your friend's grief go away, but to help them feel companioned and loved inside it.

NEW MODELS AND GOOD EXAMPLES

We cover a lot of territory in this chapter. First, I want to thank you for showing up, for wanting to help. Being with someone while they're grieving is incredibly hard work. None of this is easy. It can be uncomfortable to hear what doesn't help, especially when your heart really *is* in the right place. Throughout everything we say here, please remember that simply by wanting to be supportive, wanting to do the big, deep, heavy, hard work of loving someone inside their pain, you are doing good things.

I spend a lot of time talking about all the ways we fail to support grieving people. But it's not enough to simply state what's gone wrong. In order to move forward together, we need a new image of what grief support really is, or what it could be: an image for us to live into.

When a bone is broken, it needs a supportive cast around it to help it heal. It needs external support so it can go about the intricate, complex, difficult process of growing itself back together. Your task is to be part of that cast for your broken friend. Not to do the actual mending. Not to offer pep talks to the broken places about how they're going to be great again. Not to offer suggestions about how the bone might go about becoming whole. Your task is to simply—be there. Wrap yourself around what is broken.

Your job, should you choose to accept it, is to bear witness to something beautiful and terrible—and to resist the very human urge to fix it or make it right.

And that's hard.

LEARNING TO BEAR WITNESS

Even knowing what I know, even with what I personally experienced, even with what my students have told me again and again, I still find myself tempted to greet someone's pain with words of comfort. Those worn-out platitudes and empty condolences like "At least you gave him a good life" or "This, too, shall pass" still jump into my mind.

With everything I know about the reality of grief, what helps and what does not, I *still* want to make it better.

We all have that impulse to help. We see suffering, and we want it to stop. We see pain, and we want to intervene. We want so badly for things to be OK. That impulse to love and to soothe is human. It's part of why we're here.

We don't like to see those we love in pain.

When I ask you to respond differently, I'm not telling you to suppress that impulse to remove someone's pain. That would be impossible. What I *am* asking is that you notice your impulse to make things better, and then—don't act on it. Pause before you offer support or guidance or encouragement.

In that pause, you get to decide what the best course of action truly is. Acknowledgment of the reality of pain is usually a far better response than trying to fix it. Bearing witness is what is most called for. Does your friend need to be heard? Do they need to have the reality of the pure, utter suckage of this validated and mirrored back to them?

It seems counterintuitive, but the way to truly be helpful to someone in pain is to *let them have their pain*. Let them share the reality of how much this hurts, how hard this is, without jumping in to clean it up, make it smaller, or make it go away. That pause between the impulse to help and taking action lets you come to pain with skill, and with love. That pause lets you remember that your role is that of witness, not problem solver.

IT'S OK TO BE WEIRD ABOUT IT

It's so much harder to say, "This sucks, and there's nothing I can do. But I'm here, and I love you," rather than offer those standard words of comfort. It's so much harder, and so much more useful, loving, and kind. You can't heal someone's pain by trying to take it away from them. Acknowledgment of pain is a relief. How much softer this all becomes when we are allowed to tell the truth.

In his essay "The Gift of Presence, the Perils of Advice," author and educator Parker Palmer writes, "The human soul doesn't want to be advised or fixed or saved. It simply wants to be witnessed—to be seen, heard, and companioned exactly as it is. When we make that kind of deep bow to the soul of a suffering person, our respect reinforces the soul's healing resources, the only resources that can help the sufferer make it through."[1]

We are all, as the mystics sometimes say, part of the cloud of witnesses. In the face of pain that can't be fixed—in ourselves, in each other, in the world—we are called to bear witness. To acknowledge the reality of how much it hurts to be here, sometimes. How much life asks of us.

The role of the support team is to acknowledge and companion those in pain, not try to make it better. These are high-level skills. They aren't always easy to practice. But they *are* simple: Show up. Listen. Don't fix.

Sometimes we're clunky as we learn these new skills. That's OK.

■ ■ ■

Grieving people would much rather have you stumble through your acts of bearing witness than have you confidently assert that things are not as bad as they seem.

You can't always change pain, but you can change how you *hear* pain, how you *respond* to pain. When pain exists, let it exist. Bear witness. Make it safe for the other to say "This hurts," without rushing in to clean it up. Make space for each other.

As a support person, companionship inside what hurts is what is asked of you. By not offering solutions for what cannot be fixed, you can make things better, even when you can't make them right.

HOW DO WE BECOME PEOPLE WHO "GET IT"?

It's really hard to love someone in pain. I know.

It would be cool to have a code word, or a badge or something, that warns people of the delicate, often no-win predicament of supporting someone in pain. When Matt first died, I wanted a button that said, "Please excuse my behavior. My partner just died, and I am not myself."

It would be great if people came with care instructions: *When I feel sad, please do this. You'll know to back off when you see me do or say these things.* Unfortunately (or fortunately), we aren't mind readers. We can get better at hearing what others need by practicing attention and open communication throughout all of our lives, across all of our relationships.

Like any other skill, bearing witness to pain will get easier the more you practice it. Knowing how to respond will become more intuitive. What feels clunky and exposed will eventually become—not easy, but much, much easier.

These are skills you're always going to need. You will experience and witness pain often in your life. From smaller stressors to catastrophic losses, grief is everywhere.

The call to bear witness to pain is something we all need to learn. If you're already good at it in other areas of your life, draw on that inside your friend's grief. The more intense the pain you are called to witness, the more tempting it is to try and remove that pain. Stay still. It's OK to flinch when you see the pain we're in; just please, don't turn away from it. And don't ask us to.

ENOUGH WITH THE POETRY, WHAT ARE THE SKILLS?

It's important to talk about the deeper, larger sweep of what it means to companion someone in their grief. At the same time, we do need tangible, concrete things to *do* in the face of someone's pain. You're not meant to just—I don't know—hang out and beam love. (I mean, do that. But there are other things, too.)

Show Up, Say Something

There's a complicated dance that happens between grieving people and their support teams: most people want to be supportive, but they don't want to intrude. Or they're terrified of making things worse, so they say nothing. They pull away rather than risk an imperfect connection.

In an article for *The Guardian*, writer Giles Fraser calls this "a double loneliness"—on top of the loss of someone they love, the griever loses the connection and alliance of the people around them.[2] For fear of making things worse, people disappear and go silent just when we need them most.

I used to tell my friends that there was no way they could win. If they called me to check in too often, they were crowding me. If they didn't call often enough, they were dropping the ball, ignoring me. If I ran into someone at the grocery store and they said nothing, I felt invisible. If they wanted to talk about how I was feeling, right there in the produce section, I felt invaded.

Caring for each other is hard. It's all such a mess, at times.

The important thing to remember is that we don't need you to be perfect. It's OK—more than OK—to lead a conversation with, "I have no idea what to say, and I know I can't make this right." Or, "I want to give you space and privacy, but I'm also worried about you, and I want to check in." Claiming your discomfort allows you to show up and be present. Trying to hide your discomfort just makes things worse. From the griever's perspective, it's a huge relief to be around those who are willing to be uncomfortable and show up anyway.

If you aren't sure you should say something—ask. Err on the side of being present. Your effort really is noticed and appreciated.

Do This, Not That: A Handy Checklist

Often, when I talk about bearing witness and being with what is, people respond with, "Yeah, yeah, I can do that. But what are the things I should absolutely avoid doing?"

I understand that you want a road map. We all like concrete action steps, especially when faced with the amorphous, daunting task of supporting someone in their grief. There's an essay in the appendix that summarizes how to truly be helpful inside someone's grief, so check that out. And here are a few more points that can be made:

Don't compare griefs. Every person has experienced loss in their life, but no one else has experienced *this grief*. It's tempting to offer your own experience of grief to let the grieving person know you understand. But you don't understand. You can't. Even if your loss is empirically very similar, resist the urge to use your own experience as a point of connection.

Do: Ask questions about their experience. You can connect with someone by showing curiosity about what this is like for them. If you *have* had a similar experience, it's OK to let them know you're familiar with how bizarre and overwhelming grief can be. Just stick to indications that you know the general territory, not that you know their specific road.

Don't fact-check, and don't correct. Especially in early grief, a person's timeline and internal data sources are rather confused and wonky. They may get dates wrong, or remember things differently than they actually happened. You may have a different opinion about their relationships, or what happened when and with whom. Resist the urge to challenge or correct them.

Do: Let them own their own experience. It's not important who's "more" correct.

Don't minimize. You might think your friend's grief is out of proportion to the situation. It's tempting to correct their point of view to something you feel is more "realistic."

Do: Remember that grief belongs to the griever. Your opinions about their grief are irrelevant. They get to decide how bad things feel, just as you get to make such decisions in your own life.

Don't give compliments. When someone you love is in pain, they don't need to be reminded that they're smart, beautiful, resourceful, or a fantastically good person. Don't tell them that they're strong or brave. Grief isn't typically a failure of confidence.

Do: Remember that all those things you love about the person, all those things you admire, will help them as they move through this experience. Remind them that you're there, and that they can always lean on you when the load of grief gets too heavy to carry alone. Let them be a right awful mess, without feeling they need to show you a brave, courageous face.

Don't be a cheerleader. When things are dark, it's OK to be dark. Not every corner needs the bright light of encouragement. In a similar vein, don't encourage someone to have gratitude for the good things that still exist. Good things and horrible things occupy the same space; they don't cancel each other out.

Do: Mirror their reality back to them. When they say, "This entirely sucks," say, "Yes, it does." It's amazing how much that helps.

Don't talk about "later." When someone you love is in pain, it's tempting to talk about how great things are going to be for them in the future. Right now, in this present moment, that future is irrelevant.

Do: Stay in the present moment, or, if the person is talking about the past, join them there. Allow them to choose.

Don't evangelize (part one). "You should go out dancing; that's what helped me." "Have you tried essential oils to cheer you up?" "Melatonin always helps me sleep. You should try it." When you've found something that works for you, it's tempting to globalize that experience for everyone else. Unfortunately, unless the person specifically asked for a suggestion or information, your enthusiastic plugs are going to feel offensive and—honestly—patronizing.

Do: Trust that the person has intelligence and experience in their own self-care. If they aren't sleeping well, they've probably talked to a trusted provider, or done a simple Google search themselves. If you see them struggling, it's OK to *ask* if they'd like to hear what's helped you in the past.

Don't charge ahead with solutions (evangelizing, part two). In all things, not just in grief, it's important to get consent before giving advice or offering strategies. In most cases, the person simply needs to be heard and validated inside their pain or their challenges.

Do: Get consent. Before you offer solutions or strategies, you might borrow my friend and colleague Kate McCombs's question: "Are you wanting empathy or a strategy right now?" Respect their answer.

There are probably a million more points to make about what to do or not to do, but this list is a good starting place. It's not that all of these "don't" approaches are bad; it's simply that they aren't effective. When your goal is to support your friend, choose things that are more likely to help you achieve that goal.

HOW COME THIS ISN'T HELPING? I'M DOING ALL THE RIGHT THINGS

There's something important you need to know: sometimes, you can do everything right, and your friend will still refuse to answer your texts, show up to your party, or otherwise show that your careful attention is helping them at all.

Remember that evidence of "helping" is not in the reduction of pain; it's in knowing the grieving person feels supported and acknowledged inside their pain. But even if your intention is to support them, it still might not feel so awesome for your friend.

Your intention is important, but it's how things feel *to the grieving person* that defines how well this goes.

A long time ago, I was a sexual violence awareness educator; I spoke often about what defines sexual harassment. Some years after Matt died, I was talking to an editor friend. We'd been wondering how to describe the mismatch between what someone intends and what the grieving person experiences. I brought up the similarities between sexual harassment and grief support. My friend freaked at that comparison: "You can't tell someone who's trying to help that they're just like someone who sexually harasses!" Of course not! Sexual harassment is a completely different thing. But what I'm saying is that there are correlations there—in that the reality of the situation is defined by the *receiver* of the attention, not by the intentions of the person giving the attention. How it lands is everything. You don't have to agree with how the grieving person feels about what you've said or offered, but you do have to respect it.

Just because you mean well doesn't mean your friend receives it that way. It's always important to check. Checking in to see how things are going is an act of kindness that goes a long way in making all this better.

Remember, your goal is to truly be of service and support. That means being willing to let go of what you *think* will help and being genuinely curious—and responsive—to what your friend needs.

DON'T TAKE IT PERSONALLY (DON'T OVERWHELM WITH YOUR LOVE AND ATTENTION!)

Honestly, when it comes to grief support, I find it easier to educate the truly ignorant than I do the earnest. When someone not in my life slapped a platitude or a dismissive comment on my grief, I had no problem correcting them. But the people in my life who loved me, who so very badly wanted to help and show up and be there—they were almost too much to bear. I didn't have it in me to correct their assumptions or advice. Their attention was sometimes exhausting. In early grief, the person you love has such a low reserve of energy, they simply cannot show up for your friendship—or even for themselves—in the ways you might be used to. As I keep saying, grief is impossible. No one can win.

I've just said that you should ask your friend questions, be curious about what this is like for them, be sure to check how your actions are landing and reassess as needed. And sometimes, the more proactive you are in showing your support, in asking them for their feedback so you can be more useful, the more they seem to shut down.

Let me give you an example because this is really delicate territory: I had wonderful friends in my life before Matt died. Emotionally skilled, responsive, beautiful friends. At times, our interactions in my early grief were incredibly draining precisely *because* they wanted to know what they could do to help. They asked. And they asked. And they asked. How best to acknowledge. How best to attend. How best to ask questions, how best to give space. That pressure to tell them how to care for me was too much. It made me shy away. I simply did not have the energy to articulate my needs. Being asked, repeatedly, to offer feedback and suggestions exhausted me. At times, it made me avoid the best people in my life.

Think of it like this: your grieving person spoke a language that only one other person in the world spoke, and that person died. It's tempting to ask the grieving person to teach you that language so that you can speak it to them. No matter how much you want to speak to them, to give them back what they've lost, they can't teach you the language. Coming out of their pain to teach you syntax and grammar and vocabulary so that they can then return to their mute state is simply impossible. They cannot do it. They cannot access that part of their mind that forms lessons and offers feedback.

In a way, I'm asking you for two contradictory things: lean in and hang back. Respond to your friend, be curious and responsive to their needs. At the same time, don't ask the grieving person to do more work. Observe how things are landing for them, but in those early days, please don't expect—or demand—that they show up with their normal emotional-relational skills. They do not have them. Asking the grieving person to educate you on how best to help is simply not something they can do.

It *is* on the griever to speak up when something doesn't help. It's just unlikely that they'll do so. It's the griever's responsibility to ask for what they need. It's just unlikely that they'll do so. Draw on what you know of them, from the time before grief ripped into their lives. Use it as a compass to guide you.

Don't give up.

Here is what grieving people want you to know: We love you. We still love you, even if our lives have gone completely dark, and you can't seem to reach us. Please stay.

It's an immense relief to spend time with people who can be with the reality of grief without saying much. It's a relief to be with people who can roll with whatever comes up—from laughing maniacally to sobbing uncontrollably in the space of a few minutes. Your evenness, your steadiness of presence, is the absolutely best thing you can give.

You can't do this perfectly, and we don't expect you to. You can only aim toward more love.

For all you've done, for all you've tried to do, we appreciate your effort. Thank you.

For more information on how to support people in their grief, please refer to "How to Help a Grieving Friend" in the appendix.

PART IV
THE WAY
FORWARD

15

THE TRIBE OF AFTER

Companionship, True Hope,
and the Way Forward

Companionship, reflection, and connection are vital parts of surviving grief. As I mentioned at the beginning of this book, attachment is survival. We need each other.

Grief is already a lonely experience. It rearranges your address book: people you thought would stay beside you through anything have either disappeared or they've behaved so badly, you cut them out yourself. Even those who truly love you, who want more than anything to stay beside you, fall short of joining you here. It can feel like you lost the entire world right along with the person who died. Many grieving people feel like they're on another planet, or wish they could go to one. Somewhere there are others like them. People who understand.

We all need a place where we can tell the truth about how hard this is. We all need a place where we can share what's really going on, without feeling corrected or talked out of anything. While some friends and family can do this well, I've found that it's the community of fellow grievers that understands this best.

I've known my friend Elea for years now. We originally met online, and we didn't meet in person until long after we'd become friends. She was biking through Oregon one summer, so we decided to meet up in Seaside. When I got to Seaside, there were hundreds and hundreds of people milling around, and I had this moment of real social anxiety: "How am I going to recognize her with all these people? I've only ever seen her picture. It's not like you can just walk up to somebody and say, 'Excuse me, do you know me?'" But then I thought, *Well, she's going to have her son, Vasu, with her, so I'll just look for him. I mean, I would know that kid anywhere. I'll just look for Vasu.*

It took several seconds before I remembered: Vasu is dead. He died the same year as Matt. We never met. The only reason I know my friend Elea is because her son is dead. In fact, the only reason I know a lot of people in my life is because someone is dead.

These people are the reason I survived.

Much of what is beautiful in my life now comes from the community of other grievers: it's one of the few true gifts of loss. Every one of us would trade the community we found for the life we'd lost, and we can say so without remorse. And every one of us will fiercely love, guard, protect, and honor the others we have met here, in this life we didn't want.

> My heart is shattered, still. It is healing, slowly, in the ways that it can mend. It will always have holes in it, and maybe some other evidence of deep, painful loss, and it will never be the same as it was Before. It is both stronger and more fragile. More open, and still, closed off.
>
> Our losses are different, but I recognize yours. I hear your words and feel pain because

it all traces down to the same roots. I recognize your pain because I've felt my own. Our stories aren't the same, and the name for our loss or the relationship we grieve may be different, but I want you to know I recognize your loss as true and real.

Above all else, I'd want you to feel your loss is validated. Accepted.

I hear you.

I bow to you.

GRACE, Writing Your Grief student,
on the tribe found in the wake of her brother's death

ALONE, TOGETHER

I write and speak about grief pretty much all day, every day. My written words, my workshops, my courses—everything I do is meant to give some measure of comfort to those in pain. Sharing stories of grief from my own life and from my students' lives lets me tell you that you are not alone.

But that's where language gets tricky, especially in new grief. If an intense loss has erupted in your life, one thing you'll hear often is "You're not alone." And that isn't really true.

No matter how many times people tell you they're here for you, no matter how well they *are* here for you, no one can "do" grief with you. No one can enter into your true mind and heart and be there with you. It's not just semantics.

You are alone in your grief. You alone carry the knowledge of how your grief lives in you. You alone know all the details, the subtlety and nuance of what's happened and what's been lost. You alone know how deeply your life has been changed. You alone have to face this, inside your own heart. No one can do this with you.

That's true even if someone has had a loss similar to yours.

There's a story that makes rounds through the grief world—it's called "The Bedouin's Gazelle"; you can find one version in the book *Arab Folktales*, published by Pantheon Books. In the story, a man finds his young son dead. To soften the news for his wife, he wraps his son in a cloak and tells his wife that he has brought her a gazelle from the hunt. In order to cook it, she has to borrow a pot from a home that has never known sorrow. She goes door-to-door in her community, asking for a pot. Everyone shares a story of loss that has come to their family.

The wife returns home empty-handed, saying, "There are no pots that have not cooked a meal of sorrow." The man opens his cloak, revealing his son, and says, "It is our turn to cook meals of sorrow, for this is my gazelle."

One interpretation of this story is that everyone grieves. Whether it's this version of the folktale, or the version with the guru and the mustard seed, or any of the other versions you might find, that's the common takeaway: everyone grieves.

Not one household, not one life, is without pain.

What I hate about that interpretation is the implied second half of a statement like that: everyone grieves; therefore, your grief is not special. In other words: buck up. You don't get to be cared for in your pain because everyone is in pain. That you're not alone in experiencing loss means you have no right to such deep grief. You're asked to downgrade your pain simply because others have felt it, too.

But there's another way to look at this.

As the woman walked from house to house, not yet knowing the grief awaiting her at home, she learned the pains of others. She learned, in advance, which families had suffered the loss she was about to face. Without knowing it, she laid the groundwork for finding her own tribe within a tribe.

That journey from door to door prepared her in advance for what was to come, whispering in her ears: Meet them. Know them. You will be alone in grief—intensely alone—and *these* are the others who will know exactly what that means.

That other people have experienced pain, even pain that looks a lot like yours, is not meant as a solution to grief. It's meant to point the way to those who understand. It's meant to introduce you to your tribe.

It's meant to tell you who can hear your pain, who can stand beside you, listening, bearing witness.

That day in Seaside I expected to see Elea's son because, as part of my chosen tribe, her son is real to me. He's real because I've heard Elea's stories. Because her stories of grief sit inside her stories of love, and I know him through both things. Vasu is real, not just because I can see a picture of him happy and alive; he is real because I get to witness the story behind the story of each photograph his mother shares. I get to see the sleepless nights in my friend's face. I get to see Vasu become, as Elea wrote, "more tumor than boy." I get to see the days death came and went, and the day death came and stayed. I get to see how grief carves itself into her, shadowing each step. I get to see the love that's twinned with despair, and she gets to see mine, too. We hear each other. It hurts. And we're as comfortable with each other's pain as we are with each other's love. All of it is welcome.

And that's the thing. Everything is welcome in a community of loss. We know we're alone, and we're not alone in that. We hear each other. It doesn't fix anything, but somehow it makes it different.

Sadness is treated with human connection.

DR. PAULINE BOSS[1]

KINSHIP AND RECOGNITION

Finding others who have shared a similar depth of pain shows you those people who understand just how alone you are. Finding others lets you know that everything you're experiencing is normal, even if seemingly bizarre. Finding others who live inside this territory of grief validates the nightmare of what you already know: there are things that can never "get better."

That may seem like the opposite of helping, but for those experiencing such deep loss, having others recognize the depths of your pain is lifesaving. When someone can look at you and truly see, really recognize, the devastation at the core of your life, it changes something. It helps. It may be the only thing that does.

Companionship inside loss is one of the best indicators, not of "recovery," but of survival. Survival can be forged on your own, certainly, but it's so much easier when you travel with a wider tribe of grieving hearts.

> Death creates a family.
> I step forward into the circle
> Of mothers, fathers, daughters, sons, partners
> With tears forever in their eyes.
> Wanting to run all the way back,
> Wanting to run.
> But not running.
> I join hands with the holy mourners.
> We cannot outrun our pain so we wade into it.
> We hold each other in love and light
> And we stumble and catch each other
> And we walk without knowing why
> Or where.

The meteors stream in the moonlight
And we walk a little while together.

KATHI THOMAS ROSEN, Writing Your Grief student,
on the death of her husband, Seth

THE TRIBE OF AFTER

People in your outer world might worry that you're spending too much time on grief blogs, reading grief books, or talking with people who have lived a similar loss. That's ridiculous. We *all* look for similarity in our relationships. We naturally gravitate toward those with whom we share important things: interests, hobbies, backgrounds. Our lives are built around what we have in common. Of course you go looking for your own kind in grief. As one therapist wrote, after a loss of this magnitude, the world is split between those who know and those who do not. There is a vast divide between you and the outer world. While that divide may not always be so clear, it is now. And now is when you need your tribe.

I used to bristle at the word *tribe*. It's Internet New Age speak, and I always hate that stuff. But having lived this myself, having found my own people, and having created places for people to find each other, I can't argue with the word. We are a tribe. The Tribe of After. After death, after loss, after everyone else has moved along, the fellowship of other grievers remains.

It's easier now to find that fellowship, easier than it was when I was first widowed. Back then, there was very nearly nothing. Most online resources for grief support presumed, since I was widowed, that I was well over seventy. The few sites I found that dealt with the accidental death of a partner at a young age were heavily religious, or they tried to pour rainbows and happy endings on top of what could never be healed. Platitudes and simplistic, reductionist renderings didn't work for me before Matt died, and they were intolerable after. As an artistic, self-reflective, extra-smart, completely dorky person in what amounted to a small town, I'd often felt I didn't fit the larger world. But once Matt died? I didn't belong anywhere.

Back then, I spent endless hours on the Internet, looking for someone, anyone who sounded like me. Piece by piece, through a tangled chain of side comments and scraps of information, jumping from one (then) obscure blog to the next, I found my people.

Reading their stories, listening to the truth of their own stark, brutal pain helped me in ways nothing else could. Those people I found, the ones who stood beside me, the ones who were willing to stand beside the gaping hole that erupted in my life (and their own) and not look away or make it pretty—*they* are the reason that I survived. Their stories were the trail of bread crumbs I followed when I got lost, and I got lost a lot. That old adage, "We stand on the shoulders of giants," cannot be more true for me. I survived what was unsurvivable because of their giant hearts. Because of what we created, together. Because of the stories we told.

We reflected the broken world back to one another.

My fellow widowed people, my fellow grievers, the other broken hearts—together we knit a story of survival inside pain that can't be fixed. And we did it, simply, by telling the truth. We accepted the immoveable reality of loss. We stayed by each other inside it. We acknowledged each other's truth.

That's the power of acknowledgment: it comes up beside pain as a companion, not a solution. That's how we get through this, side by side with other devastated, broken-hearted people. Not trying to fix it. Not trying to pretty it up. But by telling the truth, and by having that truth witnessed, acknowledged, heard.

WE NEED EACH OTHER

Look, here's the deal. I never wanted to be a grief therapist. If Matt hadn't died, I would likely have left the therapy field altogether. In the days before Matt died, I told him I was tired of being in the pain business. After he died, I closed my practice; I never saw my clients again.

But grief made me lonely in ways I had never known, and I had known lonely. That loneliness drew me to search for those people who would become my tribe. That needle-in-an-invisible-haystack search, with all its dead ends and wrong turns and disappointments, is why I do the work I do now. I couldn't stand the thought of new people being thrown into the world of grief and finding nothing, hearing nothing that sounded like them.

I came back to this field because I saw how powerful connection can be. As I said earlier, writing has always been my medium. When I started this work, I wrote to give others what I myself most needed: Companionship. Acknowledgment. Survival. I wrote because my words helped. I wrote to make connection inside grief easier to find. I created things—books, blog posts, courses, workshops—because if I could do anything to make this load lighter and less lonely for anyone, one person or a thousand—I had to. What else could I possibly do?

There are a lot of words in this book taken from my Writing Your Grief courses. Over the past several years, I've had the privilege to read—and to witness—so many beautiful, horrible stories. The students who have come through these courses amaze me, over and over, with their capacity to love, their capacity to witness, their capacity to come to each other with kindness and acceptance. From their first careful days online through what is now years of support, these writers have become family for each other. They welcome each new person, each new story, with love and validation. What we've done, what we've all done, is to make space for the devastation that brings us together.

What helped me survive is what helps them survive, and is what will help you survive. It's companionship inside pain. It's the power of presence, and of bearing witness. It's not magic; it's love. Love that doesn't turn away.

You might find it through writing in the company of others. You might find it in some other forum. You might find it in real life or online. What's important is that you find a place where your loss is valued and honored and heard. When the center has been torn from your life, you need the company of others who can stand there beside the hole and not turn away.

> What a gang of grief-stricken beautiful people we are. I will miss all your voices, even the silent ones. I always noticed when a quiet voice liked a post. I wish for each of us, myself included, that we continue to reach out to those who understand loss and pain, that we find bits of comfort and ease in all our days, other groups who will listen and hear what we say, and share their own voices of loss. What a chorus we created in this group, what music we shared. I have heard paeans to life, dirges of despair, chorales of love, operas of loss. Please keep writing, each of you. I hope I listen to all your voices again, in some other group, on your blogs, or some random Internet spot. I hope the synchronicity of the universe brings our voices together again, mingled with other voices of loss from other groups here.
>
> I hope each of us finds moments to share with someone who understands what loss really

is, who helps us set a place at the table for those who are not here, who understands the pain. Salut, my friends. I bow to you all.

CHRIS GLOIN, Writing Your Grief student,
on the death of her husband, Bill

A CULTURE OF KINDNESS

Being with other people who understand the depth of your pain doesn't fix anything. As I've said a million times, some things cannot be fixed; they can only be carried. Grief like yours, love like yours, can only be carried.

Survival in grief, even eventually building a new life alongside grief, comes with the willingness to bear witness, both to yourself and to the others who find themselves inside this life they didn't see coming. Together, we create real hope for ourselves, and for one another. We need each other to survive.

I wish this for you: to find the people you belong with, the ones who will see your pain, companion you, hold you close, even as the heavy lifting of grief is yours alone. As hard as they may seem to find at times, your community is out there. Look for them. Collect them. Knit them into a vast flotilla of light that can hold you.

One of my students described our writing community as *a culture of kindness*. That is what I want for you. The good news is, there are more places to find those cultures, more opportunity to *create* those cultures, than there was even just a few short years ago. In a life you didn't ask for, in a life you didn't see coming, these small islands of true community make all the difference.

It takes work to find these places, I know. They're easier to find, but not yet easy. Read everything your heart and mind can tolerate. Read the comments (ignore the ignorant and cruel); follow the links you find there. Leave comments. Track your people through the wilderness of grief until you find their campsite, or make one of your own. I can talk in poetry about this forever, but it's the only thing I know: we find each other by becoming findable. The voices of my original tribe were a rarity back in my early days. I found them because they were willing to be found. Write, comment, connect. The more ways you find to speak your truth, the more ways your people can find you, the more ways your words can find them. Light your lantern. Raise it up. Keep looking. Keep finding.

I know it's exhausting. All of this is exhausting. And finding your tribe is the one thing I can guarantee will make this easier on you. Companionship and kinship are your survival. Even if you think it is impossible, please at least be willing to consider being found. Be fierce about it. You may be rare, but you are not the only one living a nightmare. We *are* here, and we're listening.

No one can enter the deepest heart of grief. We here, even the ones who know this magnitude of pain—we are not there with you inside your deepest grief. That intimacy is yours alone.

But together, we recognize each other and bow to the pain we see. Our hearts have held great, great sorrow. Through that pain, we can be there for each other. As our words knock on the doors of each other's hearts, we become way stations for each other.

The truth is, also: you are not alone.

 **Blessing**

> May those who weep know
> we weep with you.
> We share our different griefs together.
> The fact of loss

which tears us from community
is the very thing
bringing us together into this tribe.
We, who witness,
humanizing each the experience of another
by simple listening.
In the darkness a tiny light.
In the solitude a small voice.
In the silence, a little love.
An ear to hear,
Another heart to share,
in a still small way,
the brokenness.

RICHARD EDGAR, Writing Your Grief student,
on the loss of marriage, identity, and belonging

16

LOVE IS THE ONLY
THING THAT LASTS

How do we end a book on loss if we don't lean back on the expected happy ending? If we don't search for a tacked-on transformation, or a promise that everything will work out in the end?

I end this book with love because love is all we've got. It's neither up-note nor doom. It simply is.

We grieve because we love. Grief is part of love.

There was love in this world before your loss, there is love surrounding you now, and love will remain beside you, through all the life that is yet to come. The forms will change, but love itself will never leave. It's not enough. And it's everything.

One of my teachers spoke of the main spiritual exercise of his life as crossing back and forth over the bridge between what was before and what is now. Living in grief is continually crossing and recrossing that bridge. Survival in grief lies in finding the connection between the life that was and the life that has been thrust upon you.

In truth, we can hold on to nothing: not the physical world, not feeling states, not even our own thoughts. But love, love we can carry with us. It shifts and changes like a natural force because it is a natural force, yet somehow remains foundation, bedrock, home base. It connects what is now, to what was, to what is to come. It allows us to travel between worlds.

" Because I am held in love, this is the blessing I wish for myself: for the grace to look what has happened in the eye and accept the way it was, the way it is, the way we were, and the way we are; the grace to live with the way things are now; the courage to get up in the morning; the capacity to look at a bullfinch on the bird table or the full moon or the slant of the sun on St. Catherine's playing field behind our house and to know that there is both goodness and pain in the world, and that I am part of both.

Because I am held in love, this is my blessing for myself: to be in this space of light, however small it is, however filled with pain, each day, and to hold at bay the ravening maelstrom of chaos and darkness and disintegration of self that lurks and grabs outside this space of love. Little by little, to integrate the pain and rage and loss with love, and to overcome the darkness with light. Soft slanting sunlight, not the harsh glare of electricity, but gentle light that reveals, and also beautifies, both the whole and the broken.

Because I am held in love—in your love, Richard, and in god's love—this is my blessing for myself: to accept myself as I am, to love myself, forgive myself and allow myself to grow. To find a way of being in this world without you, sustained by love.

I. H., Writing Your Grief student,
on the death of her husband, Richard

IT'S OK THAT YOU'RE NOT OK; YOU'RE NOT MEANT TO BE OK

I think we often believe that leaning on love will fix things, like it's some mythical medicine that removes all pain, negates all hardship. That has never been love's role. Love, companionship, acknowledgment—these things come up beside you, and beneath you, to support you in your pain, not to take it away. They aren't replacements for what you've lost, and they don't make being broken any easier.

Love is brutal at times. It asks more of you than you can give. A lot of everything here, a lot of this work-of-grief, is about being strong enough to bear the weight of what love asks of you. It's about finding ways to companion yourself, to stay present to both the pain and the love that exist, side by side.

The poet Naomi Shihab Nye writes, "Love means you breathe in two countries."[1] Bridging that impossibility between the life that was and the life that is means breathing, somehow, in two countries: love exists in both, connects both.

This is going to hurt, maybe for a very long time. Broken hearts just do. The love you knew, the love you dreamed of, the love you grew and created together, that is what will get you through. It's a vast, wide raft that can't be broken or depleted. You might forget it's there sometimes, but you can always come back to it.

The entire universe can crumble (and it does), and love itself will never leave. Love is with you here, even and especially in this. Love is what sustains us. When there is nothing else to hold on to, hold on to love. Let it carry you forward.

> I believe that the world was created and approved by love, that it subsists, coheres, and endures by love, and that, insofar as it is redeemable, it can be redeemed only by love.
>
> **WENDELL BERRY,** *The Art of the Commonplace*

THE MIDDLE GROUND OF GRIEF

We have this idea that there are only two options in grief: to be sad forever and never leave the house, or to put all this sadness behind you and go on to live a fabulous life. But the reality is far broader: you are neither doomed to eternal sadness nor forced into a model of recovery that can never fit you.

There is a vast middle ground between those two extremes.

That middle ground of grief can be made only by you—you, living as best you can in alignment with what you know to be true, for yourself, with love as your guide and companion. You make that middle ground by offering yourself kindness. By refusing to give in to the dominant emotional paradigm that says your grief is a problem to be solved. By giving yourself all the time and space you need to be as broken as you are.

None of us on this grief path will return to the life, or the self, that was. Going back is simply not possible. What we can do is bow to the damaged parts, the holes blown in our lives. We can come to what remains with kindness, and with love. We can wonder what parts of ourselves survived the blast.

In a Facebook post, Anne Lamott called this "friendship with our own hearts," and that's exactly what I'm talking about. Finding your middle way inside grief is about finding friendship with your own heart, making a home inside your own heart. It's in learning to bear witness to your own pain, in treating yourself like someone you love. It's about claiming your right to be in pain, without cleaning it up or making it pretty for someone else's comfort. It's about finding those who can share this path with you, who are not afraid to see your heart in all its pain and all its grace.

Your own middle ground gets created as you experiment with grief, finding ways to stitch this experience into your life. It will change you, yes. Who you become, how you carry this loss—these things continue to unfold. The middle ground is always a work in progress. It's one that neither asks you to deny your pain, nor be forever engulfed by it. It's one that simply lets you find a home inside the reality of love, with all its beautiful and horrible parts. Held by love, inside an experience of love—it's the only place we're "safe."

> It's your life. The one you must make in the
> obliterated place that's now your world, where
> everything you used to be is simultaneously erased
> and omnipresent . . . The obliterated place is equal
> parts destruction and creation. The obliterated
> place is pitch black and bright light. It is water and
> parched earth. It is mud and it is manna. The real
> work of deep grief is making a home there.
>
> CHERYL STRAYED, *Tiny Beautiful Things*

MOVING FORWARD, TOGETHER

There isn't a lot left to say in this chapter. I know it isn't enough, this book, these words. Nothing can actually make this OK for you. My hope is that you've found companionship here, and that the exercises and practices in this book help you live the life that has been asked of you.

As best I can, I've tried to tell you the truth about grief as I know it. To give you an image to live into, a road map inside the dark. It's a story I wish I didn't have to tell, and it's the story I have.

Our hearts get broken in ways that can't be fixed. This has always been true. We must find ways to say this old truth in new ways, so that we never stop hearing it. We must speak so that others listen, so they begin to hear again. As James Baldwin writes, there isn't any other tale to tell:

Creole began to tell us what the blues were all about. They were not about anything new. He and his boys up there were keeping it new, at the risk of ruin, destruction, madness, and death, in order to find new ways to make us listen. For while the tale of how we suffer, how we are delighted and how we may triumph is never new, it always must be heard. There isn't any other tale to tell, it's the only light we've got in all this darkness.

JAMES BALDWIN, "Sonny's Blues"[2]

In telling the truth about our own hearts, we let others around us begin to find their own truth. We begin to shift the dominant paradigm that says that your grief is a problem to be solved. We get better at bearing witness to what hurts. We learn how to survive all the parts of love, even the difficult ones.

By simply stating the truth, we open conversations about grief, which are really conversations about love. We start to love one another better. We begin to overhaul the falsely redemptive storyline that has us, as a culture and as individuals, insist that there's a happy ending everywhere if only we look hard enough. We stop blaming each other for our pain, and instead, work together to change what can be changed, and withstand what can't be fixed. We get more comfortable with hearing the truth, even when the truth breaks our hearts.

In telling the truth, and in hearing the truth, we make things better, even when we can't make them right. We companion each other inside what hurts. We bear witness to each other. That's the path of love. That's what we're made for. That's the new story of bravery, the new story we need to tell.

I know you didn't ask to be part of this story. I wish that you weren't here. That you are, well—you are, and there is nothing to be done but welcome you. You're part of the change happening, both in your own heart, and in the hearts and minds of others. Simply by being here. By showing up, by staying present, by choosing to show yourself love and kindness inside what hurts.

Acknowledgment is everything, and so I end this love letter to you where we began: I'm so sorry you have need of this place, and I'm so glad you're here.

It's OK that you're not OK.

Some things cannot be fixed. They can only be carried.

May this book help you carry what is yours.

APPENDIX

How to Help a Grieving Friend

My essay on how to help a grieving friend is among the top three most shared posts I've ever written. A lot of what I've mentioned in part 3 is summarized in this essay, so I've reprinted it here. To give it to friends and family who want to help, you'll find a printable copy at refugeingrief.com/help-grieving-friend.

I've been a therapist for more than ten years. I worked in social services for the decade before that. I knew grief. I knew how to handle it in myself and how to attend to it in others. When my partner drowned on a sunny day in 2009, I learned there was a lot more to grief than I'd known.

Many people truly want to help a friend or family member who is experiencing a severe loss. Words often fail us at times like these, leaving us stammering for the right thing to say. Some people are so afraid to say or do the wrong thing, they choose to do nothing at all. Doing nothing at all is certainly an option, but it's not often a good one.

While there is no one perfect way to respond or to support someone you care about, here are some good ground rules.

1. Grief belongs to the griever.

You have a supporting role, not the central role, in your friend's grief. This may seem like a strange thing to say. So much of the advice, suggestions, and "help" given to grieving people tells them they should be doing this differently or feeling differently than they do. Grief is a very personal experience and belongs entirely to the person experiencing it. You may believe you would do things differently if it had happened to you. We hope you do not get the chance to find out. This grief belongs to your friend: follow their lead.

2. Stay present and state the truth.

It's tempting to make statements about the past or the future when your friend's present life holds so much pain. You cannot know what the future will be, for yourself or your friend—it may or may not be better "later." That your friend's life was good in the past is not a fair trade for the pain of now. Stay present with your friend, even when the present is full of pain.

It's also tempting to make generalized statements about the situation in an attempt to soothe your friend. You cannot know that your friend's loved one "finished their work here," or that they are in a "better place." These future-based, omniscient, generalized platitudes aren't helpful. Stick with the truth: This hurts. I love you. I'm here.

3. Do not try to fix the unfixable.

Your friend's loss cannot be fixed or repaired or solved. The pain itself cannot be made better. Please see #2. Do not say anything that tries to fix the unfixable, and you will do just fine. It is an unfathomable relief to have a friend who does not try to take the pain away.

4. Be willing to witness searing, unbearable pain.

To do #4 while also practicing #3 is very, very hard.

5. This is not about you.

Being with someone in pain is not easy. You will have things come up—stresses, questions, anger, fear, guilt. Your feelings will likely be hurt. You may feel ignored and unappreciated. Your friend cannot show up for their part of the relationship very well. Please don't take it personally, and please don't take it out on them. Please find your own people to lean on at this time—it's important that you be supported while you support your friend. When in doubt, refer to #1.

6. Anticipate, don't ask.

Do not say, "Call me if you need anything," because your friend will not call. Not because they do not need, but because identifying a need, figuring out who might fill that need, and then making a phone call to ask is light years beyond their energy levels, capacity or interest. Instead, make concrete offers: "I will be there at 4:00 p.m. on Thursday to bring your recycling to the curb," or "I will stop by each morning on my way to work and give the dog a quick walk." Be reliable.

7. Do the recurring things.

The actual, heavy, real work of grieving is not something you can do (see #1), but you can lessen the burden of "normal" life requirements for your friend. Are there recurring tasks or chores that you might do? Things like walking the dog, refilling prescriptions, shoveling snow, and bringing in the mail are all good choices. Support your friend in small, ordinary ways—these things are tangible evidence of love.

Please try not to do anything that is irreversible—like doing laundry or cleaning up the house—unless you check with your friend first. That empty soda bottle beside the couch may look like trash, but may have been left there by their husband just the other day. The dirty laundry may be the last thing that smells like her. Do you see where I'm going here? Tiny little normal things become precious. Ask first.

8. Tackle projects together.

Depending on the circumstance, there may be difficult tasks that need tending—things like casket shopping, mortuary visits, the packing and sorting of rooms or houses. Offer your assistance and follow through with your offers. Follow your friend's lead in these tasks. Your presence alongside them is powerful and important; words are often unnecessary. Remember #4: bear witness and be there.

9. Run interference.

To the new griever, the influx of people who want to show their support can be seriously overwhelming. What is an intensely personal and private time can begin to feel like living in a fish bowl. There might be ways you can shield and shelter your friend by setting yourself up as the designated point person—the one who relays information to the outside world, or organizes well-wishers. Gatekeepers are really helpful.

10. Educate and advocate.

You may find that other friends, family members, and casual acquaintances ask for information about your friend. You can, in this capacity, be a great educator, albeit subtly. You can normalize grief with responses like, "She has better moments and worse moments and will for quite some time. An intense loss changes every detail of your life." If someone asks you about your friend a little further down the road, you might say things like, "Grief never really stops. It is something you carry with you in different ways."

11. Love.

Above all, show your love. Show up. Say something. Do something. Be willing to stand beside the gaping hole that has opened in your friend's life, without flinching or turning away. Be willing to not have any answers. Listen. Be there. Be present. Be a friend. Be love. Love is the thing that lasts.

NOTES

Chapter 3: It's Not You, It's Us: Our Models of Grief Are Broken

1. Brené Brown, *Rising Strong: The Reckoning. The Rumble. The Revolution* (New York: Spiegel and Grau, 2015).

Chapter 4: Emotional Illiteracy and the Culture of Blame

1. For more on the origins of victim blaming, see Adrienne LaFrance, "Pompeii and the Ancient Origins of Blaming the Victim," *The Atlantic,* October 2, 2015, theatlantic.com/technology/archive/2015/10/did-the-people-at-pompeii-get-what-they-deserved/408586/.
2. Cheryl Strayed, *Tiny Beautiful Things: Advice on Love and Life from Dear Sugar* (New York: Vintage, 2012), 145.
3. Ibid.
4. Barbara Ehrenreich, *Smile or Die: How Positive Thinking Fooled America and the World* (London: Granta Books, 2010); also her article, "Smile! You've Got Cancer," *The Guardian,* January 1, 2010, www.theguardian.com/lifeandstyle/2010/jan/02/cancer-positive-thinking-barbara-ehrenreich.
5. Ibid.

Chapter 5: The New Model of Grief

1. Pauline Boss, "The Myth of Closure," interview with Krista Tippett, On Being, June 23, 2016, onbeing.org/programs/Pauline-boss-the-myth-of-closure/.

Chapter 6: Living in the Reality of Loss

1. Ground rules for living in grief: see the Rules of Impact at my website, Refuge in Grief, refugeingrief.com/rules-at-impact-how-to-survive-early-grief.

Chapter 8: How (and Why) to Stay Alive

1. See Mirabai Starr, "Softening into the Pain" (blog entry), January 12, 2011, https://mirabaistarr.com/softening-into-the-pain/.

Chapter 9: What Happened to My Mind? Dealing with Grief's Physical Side Effects

1. For more on neurobiology and attachment, see Thomas Lewis, Fari Amini, and Richard Lannon, *A General Theory of Love* (New York: Vintage, 2001).
2. James Hillman, *The Dream and the Underworld* (New York: Harper & Row, 1979).

Chapter 11: What Does Art Have to Do with Anything?

1. The practice of writing below the line comes from one of my first writing teachers, Eunice Scarfe, of Edmonton, Alberta.

Chapter 12: Find Your Own Image of "Recovery"

1. Samira Thomas, "In Praise of Patience," *Aeon*, May 12, 2016, aeon.co/essays/how-patience-can-be-a-better-balm-for-trauma-than-resilience.
2. Ibid.

Chapter 14: Rallying Your Support Team: Helping Them Help You

1. Parker Palmer, "The Gift of Presence, the Perils of Advice," On Being, April 27, 2016, onbeing.org/blog/the-gift-of-presence-the-perils-of-advice/.
2. Giles Fraser, "We Cannot Fix People's Grief, Only Sit with Them, in Their Darkness," *The Guardian*, April 14, 2016, theguardian.com/commentisfree/belief/2016/apr/14/we-cannot-fix-peoples-grief-only-sit-with-them-in-their-darkness.

Chapter 15: The Tribe of After: Companionship, True Hope, and the Way Forward

1. Pauline Boss, "The Myth of Closure," interview with Krista Tippett, On Being, June 23, 2016, onbeing.org/programs/Pauline-boss-the-myth-of-closure/.

Chapter 16: Love Is the Only Thing That Lasts

1. Naomi Shihab Nye, *Words Under the Words: Selected Poems* (Portland, OR: Eighth Mountain Press, 1994).
2. James Baldwin, *Going to Meet the Man: Stories* (New York: Vintage Books, 1995).

RESOURCES

It's still tough to find good resources when you're grieving. The support landscape is getting better, but it's not yet awesome. The organizations listed below are among my few favorites.

For dealing with grief in families with children, there's no better place than the Dougy Center. They're international experts in children's grief, and some of the only professionals invited in after large-scale natural or human-made disasters. Find them at dougy.org.

The MISS Foundation offers support and resources for people grieving the death of a child at any age. See missfoundation.org.

Soaring Spirits International hosts a blog written by several different writers, each living with the loss of a spouse or partner. The foundation also holds several weekend conferences for widowed people, with a large percentage of attendees widowed under age fifty. Look for Camp Widow on the website soaringspirits.org. From their resources page, you can find links to lots of other services for widowed individuals and grieving families.

Modern Loss is a great site, especially for younger and midlife adults. They cover a variety of losses via guest posts and essays. If you're a writer, you might also consider submitting your own work. Find them at modernloss.com.

Glow in the Woods is a site for babylost families. They're an amazing resource both for companionship inside loss and for information on coping with the physical and emotional realities of neonatal and postpartum death. Visit glowinthewoods.com.

The Liz Logelin Foundation awards funds to families when a parent dies. Information on grants and resources for grieving families can be found at thelizlogelinfoundation.org.

ABOUT THE AUTHOR

Megan Devine is a writer, speaker, and grief advocate. She travels the world encouraging people to speak the truth about their pain, and learn to really listen without jumping in to fix each other's broken hearts. She lives with an ever-changing band of beasts on a tiny plot of land near the highway in Oregon.

ABOUT SOUNDS TRUE

Sounds True is a multimedia publisher whose mission is to inspire and support personal transformation and spiritual awakening. Founded in 1985 and located in Boulder, Colorado, we work with many of the leading spiritual teachers, thinkers, healers, and visionary artists of our time. We strive with every title to preserve the essential "living wisdom" of the author or artist. It is our goal to create products that not only provide information to a reader or listener, but that also embody the quality of a wisdom transmission.

For those seeking genuine transformation, Sounds True is your trusted partner. At SoundsTrue.com you will find a wealth of free resources to support your journey, including exclusive weekly audio interviews, free downloads, interactive learning tools, and other special savings on all our titles.

To learn more, please visit SoundsTrue.com/freegifts or call us toll-free at 800.333.9185.